PRAISE FOR *ENGAGEMENT*

The brilliance of the Best of the Best series is in the way it opens up so many new possibilities around some of education's most heavily used (yet often poorly understood) buzzwords: progress, feedback and, now, engagement. Incisive, provocative thinking from a wide range of experts is smartly contextualised through practical and inventive strategies devised by Wallace and Kirkman – find what resonates with you, and give it a try!

Helen Mulley, Editor, *Teach Secondary*

Drawing on digestible anecdotes, observations and thinking from some of the leading education experts involved in inspiring teaching and learning, Isabella Wallace and Leah Kirkman galvanise teachers to improve their practice by offering practical strategies that can be easily utilised through subtle changes to working routines.

Engagement would be a perfect accompaniment to a series of staff development sessions, within which the contributors' ideas could be explored and related to the school's teaching and learning culture and used to help rouse pupils to attain improved outcomes.

Colin Hill, Founder and Director, UKEdChat

This nifty little book is a hugely uplifting read – a lucky dip of entertaining, no-nonsense theory and practical strategies. It exudes warmth as the contributors share their wisdom, innovation and advice in a humorous, unthreatening and realistic way, making it a genuinely enjoyable read.

Engagement manages to appeal to both the NQT and the senior leader, and quite rightly refocuses our attention on what really matters. By distributing copies in our staff book club we have provided first-class professional development for less than the cost of a conference ticket!

Louise Laming, Head Teacher, Lincoln Castle Academy

The dynamic duo – Isabella and Leah – are at it again. This concise gold mine features an A-list of education's most prominent voices and enables them to share their ideas and wisdom on the topic of engagement. In this volume you'll find an array of practical strategies and advice to help teachers consolidate engagement in the classroom, all of which are applicable across the curriculum and in every phase.

There is something for everyone in *Engagement*, making it an essential read for both new and experienced educationalists.

**Rebecca Poorhady,
Learning and Development Organiser, Midlands region,
Association of Teachers and Lecturers**

ENGAGEMENT

ENGAGEMENT

ISABELLA WALLACE AND LEAH KIRKMAN

Crown House Publishing Limited
www.crownhouse.co.uk

First published by

Crown House Publishing Ltd
Crown Buildings, Bancyfelin, Carmarthen, Wales, SA33 5ND, UK
www.crownhouse.co.uk

and

Crown House Publishing Company LLC
PO Box 2223, Williston, VT 05495, USA
www.crownhousepublishing.com

British Library Cataloguing-in-Publication Data
A catalogue entry for this book is available from the British Library.

Print ISBN 978-178583247-5
Mobi ISBN 978-178583329-8
ePub ISBN 978-178583330-4
ePDF ISBN 978-178583331-1

LCCN 2017964359

Printed and bound in the UK by
Gomer Press, Llandysul, Ceredigion

PREFACE

When some of us started teaching many moons ago, our initial preparatory training and the subsequent professional development we received didn't really expose us to a wealth of educational thinkers, theorists or researchers. There were the staples – perhaps a pinch of Piaget here or a dusting of Dewey there ... But times are changing. Today – right now – we are witnessing the dawn of a very different informational landscape. Important, knowledgeable voices in education ring out from all directions. Not simply political ones, but the voices of experts and practitioners who have devoted significant time in their lives to the education of young people or examining the issues that surround it.

This is a wonderful development. But teachers are notoriously busy. Sometimes those of us working in education are *so* busy that being faced with such an array of diverse opinions and theories can feel overwhelming rather than helpful. It can be hard to see how we might apply ideas to our own schools and classrooms, our own year groups or subjects.

The purpose of the Best of the Best series is to bring together – for the first time – the most influential voices in one accessible format. A compendium of the most useful advice from the most celebrated educationalists. Each title in the series focuses on a different all-important theme and features a comprehensive collection of brief and accessible contributions from the most eminent names in education internationally. In these books you have it straight from the horse's mouth. But that's not all: in close liaison with those experts, we have developed practical, realistic, cross-curricular and cross-phase ways to make the most of these important insights *in the classroom*.

We've translated theory into practice for you, and every edition in the series is written for teachers, by teachers. Of course, if a particular concept takes your fancy and you have time to delve a little deeper, all of our experts have pointed you in the right direction for further reading. And all of a sudden the continuing professional development (CPD) voyage seems a little less overwhelming. Contented sigh.

To top it all off, the wonderful Teacher Development Trust has outlined a collaborative group approach for teachers to read the book together and try out the ideas, as well as providing helpful guidance to school leaders on how to set up CPD around the book's theme for maximum impact.

Have a breathtaking adventure discovering the best tips from the best people, and don't forget to look out for other titles in the collection!

Isabella Wallace and Leah Kirkman

ACKNOWLEDGEMENTS

As always, we owe a huge thank you to the great educationalists who have taken time out of their busy lives to share their ideas and findings with us in this third book in the Best of the Best series.

Tremendous thanks also to David, Rosalie, Tabitha and the whole Crown House Publishing team, who continue to help us bring together the best authorities on education from all over the world. It was a project that others felt was too ambitious to achieve, but with you believing in us, we did it!

We are honoured that David Weston and the Teacher Development Trust have collaborated with us once again and offered their guidance at the end of the book.

Finally, we'd like to thank the teachers and lecturers of our youth. Some of you showed us how to engage our brains even when the topic was of little personal interest, and some of you showed us how even an interesting topic can be rendered dull with the wrong approach. We are extremely grateful to you all!

CONTENTS

INTRODUCTION

As fans of *Star Trek* may well remember, when Captain Jean-Luc Picard pointed his finger and gave the order, 'Engage!' his command was met with swift compliance. In education it isn't so easy. Engagement can't be compelled and will always be contingent on the complexities of motivation, whether of the teacher or the learners. Indeed, several of the Best of the Best contributors in this volume – such as Sir Tim Brighouse – argue that it is teacher engagement which is the key to successful learning. Such engagement can be best facilitated in schools, suggests Vic Goddard, by encouraging activities such as professional dialogue between staff; and Richard Gerver argues that an institution's high expectations and assumption of excellence will encourage in its teachers a sense of professional engagement and empowerment. Similarly, Andy Cope – with echoes of the psychologist Eric Fromm – advises that teachers should focus on how they wish 'to be' in order to achieve the energy and empowerment to engage more effectively with their to-do list; and Professor Bill Lucas takes this responsibility for engagement a step further by focusing on ways that schools can encourage parental engagement.

The specific link between teacher engagement and learner motivation is argued persuasively by several contributors. Ian Gilbert, for example, stresses the need for teachers to behave in a way that makes our learners feel as though we like them. Professor Susan Wallace and Sue Cowley, too, argue that building a positive teacher–learner relationship is an essential step towards improving learner engagement.

So how do we recognise learner engagement and what else can we do to encourage it? An important point made by Sue Cowley and Dr Debra Kidd is that engagement is by no means synonymous with simply 'having fun'. Indeed, as Ian Gilbert points out, the opposite of 'boring' in a learning context should be 'challenging'. The challenge must, however, as Andy Griffith argues, be one which learners feel is achievable if they are to become properly involved and absorbed in the state of 'flow'. Conrad Wolfram, writing specifically about motivation in maths, suggests that in addition to being achievable, the challenge must be carefully chosen: not any old abstract problem but one which learners feel motivated to solve. Sue Cowley and Debra Kidd put this another way, arguing that motivation to remain engaged will always be contingent on learners being able to see the relevance, purpose and value of what they are being asked to do. Paul Dix builds on this notion, illustrating for us the importance of finding ways to engage learners' natural curiosity with an element of anticipation, surprise or even some mild jeopardy.

A number of the contributors in this book suggest very specific strategies for optimising learner engagement. John Davitt, for example, encourages the idea of engagement as 'doing' – where learners are asked to demonstrate understanding in a variety of ways and through means other than simply writing; while Mike Gershon suggests using discussion to help learners refine and articulate their ideas before they engage in a writing task. Susan Wallace, on the other hand, focuses on teacher behaviour, suggesting that one of the most effective ways of encouraging engagement is for the teacher to model the desired attitude by presenting themselves as enthusiastic and highly motivated.

A final theme that emerges among the experts' chapters is focusing on engagement in terms of appropriate learner behaviour and attitudes. Professor Mick Waters argues that in this context a gentle 'nudging' towards improved behaviour – for example, through the awarding of points – will prove more effective than the use of sanctions or shaming. Dr Bill Rogers, too, advocates a non-confrontational approach and illustrates how the teacher's verbal communications with the class can be more effective in encouraging appropriate behaviour and focus when they are descriptive and assertive rather than imperative and confrontational. Phil Beadle, however, raises the question of whether levels of engagement are largely contingent on geography and environment, suggesting that inner city schools may be facing the problem of learner disengagement on a scale not experienced elsewhere. He points out that, in the absence of other sources of motivation, the learning experience needs to be enjoyable if engagement is to be achieved.

From this compendium of expert voices, then, three important themes emerge about engagement: that teachers' engagement and positive example should be seen as a prerequisite for establishing learner motivation; that learners' interest needs to be actively engaged, whether by meaningful challenge or by tapping into their natural curiosity; and that an expectation of appropriate behaviour must precede expectations of engagement. And, of course, as Ian Gilbert points out, to encourage engaged behaviour we need first to banish classroom boredom. In these pages you will find many practical suggestions of ways to do exactly that.

CHAPTER 1

TEACHERS: OUR MOST POWERFUL RESOURCE

SIR TIM BRIGHOUSE

SIR TIM BRIGHOUSE started his career as a teacher in secondary schools and later became an administrator, being chief education officer for ten years in both Oxfordshire and Birmingham local authorities. He was also head of the education department at Keele University where he founded the Centre for Successful Schools. He ended his career as commissioner for London schools where he ran the London Challenge.

The best advice I ever received on how to improve teaching, and therefore schools, came from the American educator Judith Little, whose research concluded that you knew you were in a good school when the following four characteristics were present:

1. Teachers talk about teaching.

2. Teachers observe each other teach.

3. Teachers plan, organise and evaluate together.

4. Teachers teach each other.

My reason for liking these findings is because you can easily see how you can increase or decrease the likelihood of these four things happening. For example, if the agendas of meetings are packed with administrative imperatives rather than discussion of pedagogy or curricular subtleties to aid learning, then meetings are wasted time. Conversely, starting primary staff meetings in different classrooms, with the host analysing where they are with optimising the environment for learning, will promote valuable debate – as would an agenda item where, in turns (one member per meeting), staff outline the book they are reading with their class and why it works for that age group.

Or, at secondary level, the senior leadership team (SLT) taking over the teaching of a department for a day could enable the staff to be released to visit a department in another school.

My advice, therefore, would be to have a session where all staff look at the four characteristics outlined by Judith Little and share ideas of how, with minimal effort, school practices could be adjusted to make them happen more often.

FURTHER READING

Brighouse, Tim and Woods, David (2013). *The A-Z of School Improvement: Principles and Practice* (London: Bloomsbury Education).

PRACTICAL STRATEGIES

As Sir Tim Brighouse points out, developing any aspect of teaching is usually best done through collaboration with other teachers. To explore the concept of engagement in your own classroom and across your school, try initiating some of the following practices with your colleagues.

TEACHERS TALK ABOUT TEACHING

▪ Organise a teaching and learning event or TeachMeet[1] at your school where you invite teachers from your own and other establishments to come and share useful ideas for pupil engagement that they have tried and tested in their classrooms. The traditional TeachMeet approach is to give each contributor approximately three minutes to present their idea. This allows attendees to hear an impressive quantity of suggestions and they can consult with presenters afterwards to find out more about the techniques.

▪ Set up a weekly 'bring a problem to breakfast' meeting. This is where breakfast is provided for staff who wish to start the day by sharing a difficulty they are experiencing

---

1 An organised meeting for teachers to share good practice and practical innovations with each other.

in their teaching and then obtaining helpful suggestions from other colleagues for addressing that problem.

- Launch a 'listening ear' initiative, whereby there is a different volunteer available in the staffroom at the end of each day. This volunteer's role is to offer a friendly ear and informal counsel to any colleague who wishes to debrief the events of their working day before they go home.

- Create an idea-sharing area in the staffroom. Ask colleagues to post details of something they have tried that worked well. Preferably this should be a technique that they feel could be used effectively in a variety of curriculum areas, and it could be accompanied by a photograph. This display is likely to attract a lot of readers. It is a wonderful way of encouraging a culture of innovation and of taking pleasure and pride in the job.

A and B meet to discuss what aspects of their own teaching they would like to focus on

They co-plan A's lesson

B joins A's lesson and makes notes on things she finds interesting and on points for discussion

A and B meet up to debrief the lesson

They co-plan B's lesson

TEACHERS OBSERVE EACH OTHER TEACH

■ Whenever you are going to observe a colleague teach, and no matter the capacity in which you are observing them, help them to feel that they own their own observation experience by asking them how you can be most helpful during the lesson. Questions like, 'How can I make this process most helpful to you?', 'Is there a particular aspect of your teaching you'd like me to focus on?' and 'Are there specific learners you'd like me to watch and feed back on?' are useful when emphasising the developmental intent of your observation.

TEACHERS PLAN, ORGANISE AND EVALUATE TOGETHER

■ Trial a peer coaching model such as the one illustrated in the diagram below. Teachers of the same or different subjects/year groups can be paired up. The act of

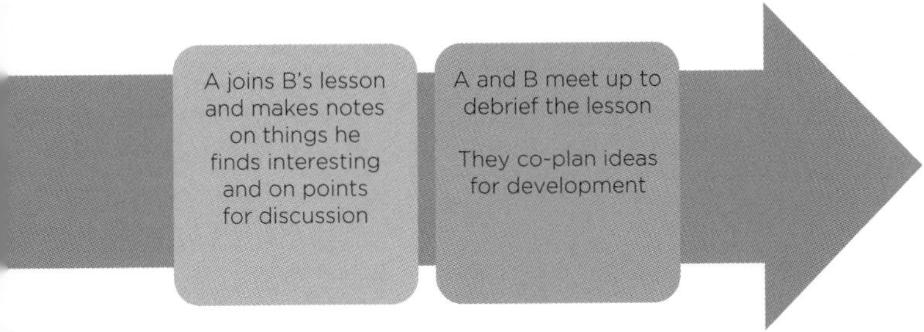

A joins B's lesson and makes notes on things he finds interesting and on points for discussion

A and B meet up to debrief the lesson

They co-plan ideas for development

co-planning, analysing impact and debriefing can be an extremely insightful experience, and is an excellent way to get colleagues engaging in meaningful discussion about pedagogy. It also builds collegial relationships and inspires high levels of trust across a staff team.

TEACHERS TEACH EACH OTHER

■ For a fun staff meeting that keeps the focus on teaching and learning, apply the concept of 'speed-dating' to your meeting agenda. Ask every member of staff to bring a practical, realistic strategy for engagement to the meeting. Half the staff should stand around the edge of the room, facing in, and the remaining teachers should go and stand opposite a colleague, forming an inner circle. Each teacher has one minute to share their idea with their partner. When a bell or other auditory cue sounds, the outer circle remains still and the inner circle moves one place clockwise. Now each teacher has a new partner and they each take a further minute to share their idea again. This process continues until all staff have encountered a wide range of ideas and spoken with a great number of colleagues they might not normally talk to.

CHAPTER 2

THE LANGUAGE OF DISCIPLINE

DR BILL ROGERS

DR BILL ROGERS is a teacher, education consultant and author. He conducts INSETs and seminar programmes across Australia, New Zealand, Europe and the UK in the areas of behaviour management, effective teaching, stress management, colleague support and teacher welfare. He has also worked extensively as a mentor-coach in classrooms, team-teaching in challenging classes in Australia and the UK. Bill Rogers read theology at Ridley College, Melbourne, then psychology, philosophy and education at Melbourne University and went on to major in education. He is a Fellow of the Australian College of Educators, an Honorary Life Fellow of Leeds Trinity University and an Honorary Fellow at the Graduate School of Education, Melbourne University.

It's day one, the first lesson with a restless Year 7 class. Some students are calling out, some still chatting, some fiddling with *objets d'art* on their tables. The bell has just gone for this first lesson. The teacher is acutely aware that how she disciplines now will have a significant effect on her ongoing relationship with this class and on how she establishes a positive, cooperative learning culture (Rogers, 2015).

She scans the faces of her class. She is seeking to communicate a sense of calmness and expectation. Most students begin to settle and relax. To those still chatting she says, 'A number of students are still chatting ... ' A brief descriptive cue. She gives a brief tactical pause for focus (...). She adds, 'You need to be facing this way and listening ... Thanks.' The 'thanks' is more expectational than 'please' – it is not a request.

She doesn't ask unhelpful questions like: 'Why are you still talking?', 'Can you please listen?', 'Are you supposed to be calling out?' Nor does she use negative directions: 'Don't talk while I'm teaching,' 'Don't call out please.'

To the two lads distractingly playing with the window blind cords, 'Bilal ... Dean ... You're fiddling with the blinds. It's really distracting.' This descriptive cue raises their behaviour awareness. She adds a behaviour direction: 'Leave the blinds and face this way ... Thanks.' She focuses on the expected behaviour,

...ather than on the negative behaviour: 'Don't fiddle with the blinds ...' or 'Why are you ...?'

She refocuses her attention on the rest of the class. This gives take-up time to the boys, conveying her expectation of cooperation. She tactically ignores the sigh and rolling of eyes of one of the boys.

The class is basically settled. She says, 'Good morning.' She will not greet her class until they have returned the calmness and expectation she conveys. She will not talk through or over their chatting or calling out. She will cue the distracting students with a brief, respectful, descriptive/directional focus: 'Melissa ... Chantelle ... You're chatting. You need to be facing this way and listening ... Thanks.' When students sigh, roll their eyes or sulk on receipt of a discipline cue, she will tactically ignore their secondary behaviour, keeping the focus on the primary behaviour (or issue) at that point. She knows this will set a positive precedent.

Later, in the on-task phase of the lesson, she moves around the classroom giving encouragement, refocusing and supporting individuals. She notices a couple of students surreptitiously playing with their smartphones. She walks over and greets them, 'How's the work going ...?' She is task-focused; she doesn't say, 'Right, give me the phones – now.' After refocusing on the learning task, she gives the girls a directed choice: 'The phones need to be off and away in your bags, or you can leave them on my desk until the end of the lesson.'

One of the girls frowningly whinges, 'But we weren't even using them.' The teacher tactically ignores this sulky secondary tone and refocuses on the primary issue by briefly and partially agreeing, 'Even if you weren't …' (not 'I don't care if you weren't …') – and then repeats the directed choice. She doesn't argue or try to defend the school rule. She walks away (take-up time) to convey her expectation of cooperation.

If, after reasonable take-up time, the girls' phones are still out, she will return and clarify the consequences: 'If you choose not to put the phone(s) away, I'll have to ask you to stay back in your own time.' She puts the responsibility where it belongs – on the student.

She is consciously aware of avoiding unnecessary confrontation and power struggles. She chooses her language of discipline to enable student ownership and cooperation.

This teacher is employing her language of discipline in a way that is least intrusive and conveys a positive, expectant, respectful intent. Where possible, she will use appropriate choices.

On occasion, she will need to use decisive, assertive statements, as when some students swear or use sexist, homophobic or misogynistic language: 'I don't make comments about your body (or clothing or sexuality or …).' If the student says, 'I'm only joking!' she will make clear, 'It's not a joke and I expect to stop – now.' If a student continues with any persistently disruptive behaviour she will employ the school's time-out procedures.

She has started to build trust and enable her students to own their behaviour in a way that considers others' rights and needs. A significant feature of that relational trust is her language of discipline.

FURTHER READING

Rogers, Bill (1990). *You Know the Fair Rule: Strategies for Making the Hard Job of Discipline in Schools Easier* (Camberwell, VIC: Australian Council for Education Research).

Rogers, Bill (2011). *The Essential Guide to Managing Teacher Stress: Practical Skills for Teachers* (London: Pearson Education).

Rogers, Bill (2015). *Classroom Behaviour: A Practical Guide to Effective Teaching, Behaviour Management and Colleague Support* (London: Pearson Education).

Rogers, Bill and McPherson, Elizabeth (2014). *Behaviour Management with Young Children: Crucial First Steps with Children 3–7 Years* (London: SAGE).

PRACTICAL STRATEGIES

Whether learners remain focused, engaged and motivated to work in the classroom can depend very significantly on the attitude and expectations conveyed by the teacher. Research suggests that our characteristic discipline language has a significant effect on the cooperation and goodwill of our students (Rogers, 1990, 2011, 2015). The following is a summary of the effective strategies that the teacher uses in Bill Rogers' scenario above.

DESCRIPTIVE CUEING

■ When learners are off-task and wasting valuable time, it is best to respond to this undesirable behaviour in a measured way, as this prevents us from reacting emotionally. A useful strategy is to simply state what the student is doing and describe the effect it is having – for example, 'James, you are looking at your phone. It's disadvantaging your group because they're a player short.' This raises the student's awareness of their learning behaviour while avoiding unnecessary confrontation. The teacher is also clearly stating the reason for their intervention: 'It's disadvantaging your group.' This is a useful preventative strategy to use before a situation escalates.

BEHAVIOUR DIRECTIONS

■ To motivate a learner to focus and work hard, our
instructions should be positive ones. 'Put all distractions
away and see if you can answer questions 1–4 in the next
ten minutes' is significantly more motivational than, 'Stop
playing with your phone' or 'Why have you got your phone
out again?' A clear, positively phrased instruction reduces
the potential for time-wasting retorts from a learner, such
as, 'I'm not playing with it!' or 'Because I need to phone
home!'

TAKE-UP TIME

■ Following a positive behaviour direction, don't expect
students to switch immediately into mega-motivated
mode before your very eyes. A difficult student may be
less likely to comply under your confrontational glare
simply because it makes them feel more combative.
Instead, turn your attention back to your teaching activity.
This wordlessly communicates your confidence that the
student will do as asked, just as the phrase 'thank you'
powerfully assumes compliance. You may find it's useful
to temporarily move away from the student entirely –
circulating around the rest of the class, monitoring levels

of understanding and engagement, while the student in question makes best use of their take-up time.

TACTICAL IGNORING

It is important that when dealing with one demotivated student, we do it in a way which causes the least disruption possible to the class's learning. One demotivated, off-task student can quickly turn into a situation where the entire class is off-task and staring if we use an intervention that draws mass attention to the undesirable behaviour. Since we are prioritising pupil progress, we may choose to make use of a non-verbal behaviour like tactical ignoring to show students where the focus of our attention is – on the learning. After you have dealt with a student's off-task behaviour, they may well exhibit less disruptive secondary behaviours such as rolling their eyes or sighing loudly. It can be useful, in these moments, to give them their 'diva dignity' and tactically ignore this secondary feature of their behaviour, thereby keeping the focus of attention directed on the initial behaviour that was genuinely impacting negatively on teaching and learning.

VIC GODDARD is proud to be a council estate boy from South London, but therefore suffers the curse of being a Crystal Palace fan. If you caught any of *Educating Essex* he was probably the one crying.

From a young age Vic wanted to be a PE teacher, and following his degree course in Chichester enjoyed two years working on the south coast at Angmering School learning from two of the best PE teachers you could ever wish to meet. During this time Vic realised that he wanted to be a head teacher and set himself the target of being a head by 40 and on the golf course by 50! This led to him moving on from jobs, sad to leave but determined to make the next career step. Four years in Cheam and then a three-year stint working in an international school in Cairo followed, where he took on the role of head of faculty.

On returning to the UK, Vic was fortunate to work with a truly inspiring head teacher, Kevin Sadler, in his first SLT role, and in five years went from assistant head to head at Passmores School (now Academy) in Harlow. Vic feels privileged to be a head teacher and is humbled every day that parents/carers are willing to trust him to educate their children.

CHAPTER 3

STARTING FROM THE BOTTOM UP

VIC GODDARD

A few years ago it became obvious to me that, with the limited timetable I teach, I was losing credibility in leading teaching and learning. Who was I to stand up and espouse a certain type of pedagogy when I was in front of colleagues who were doing it many more times than I was every day?

We then appointed leaders of pedagogy to work across the school to develop teaching and learning. The 'ped leaders' appointed are from a variety of subjects and levels of experience. We have since seen quite remarkable progress in the development of teachers' professional practice at Passmores. The staff-led teaching and learning communities (TLCs) have proven to be a catalyst for improvement, but also a much more motivating experience than the whole-school SLT-led CPD sessions. The development of a dialogue between staff, who feel able to share their successes when trying something new as well as being honest when things do not quite go according to plan, has noticeably reinvigorated staff who have been teaching for some time.

This bottom-up approach has led to the development of our teaching and learning website and the active engagement of students in the development of classroom practice. On the school website we publish blogs from students and staff as well as the 'Passmores Buzz' – an area where staff share lessons that have gone well with particular classes.

The fact that we have students and staff working together on the co-construction of lessons – and specifically on the use of technology to enhance, not overpower, the learning experience – has led to an active dialogue that has been both challenging and motivating.

FURTHER READING

Beadle, Phil (2010). *How to Teach* (Carmarthen: Crown House Publishing).

Berry, Jill (2016). *Making the Leap: Moving from Deputy to Head* (Carmarthen: Crown House Publishing).

Christodoulou, Daisy (2016). *Making Good Progress? The Future of Assessment for Learning* (Oxford: Oxford University Press).

Hendrick, Carl (2017). *What Does This Look Like in the Classroom? Bridging the Gap Between Research and Practice* (Woodbridge: John Catt Educational).

Myatt, Mary (2016). *High Challenge, Low Threat: How the Best Leaders Find the Balance* (Woodbridge: John Catt Educational).

O'Brien, Jarlath (2016). *Don't Send Him in Tomorrow: Shining a Light on the Marginalised, Disenfranchised and Forgotten Children of Today's Schools* (Carmarthen: Independent Thinking Press).

Pieper, Kenny (2016). *Reading for Pleasure: A Passport to Everywhere* (Carmarthen: Independent Thinking Press).

Smith, Jim (2017). *The Lazy Teacher's Handbook: How Your Students Learn More When You Teach Less* (Carmarthen: Independent Thinking Press).

Tierney, Stephen (2016). *Liminal Leadership: Building Bridges Across the Chaos ... Because We're Standing on the Edge* (Woodbridge: John Catt Educational).

PRACTICAL STRATEGIES

The experience of CPD is important. We can't expect to easily engage students in their learning if we, as teachers, are not 'engaged learners' ourselves. Vic Goddard emphasises how involving teachers fully in their own development is crucial. If people feel that CPD is being done 'to' them, and they don't feel personally invested in the experience, it is very unlikely to have the desired effect. Try some of the following strategies to engage your colleagues in an active dialogue about teaching and learning.

WORKING ACROSS THE SCHOOL TO DEVELOP TEACHING

■ To investigate a particular aspect of teaching, set up an action research group whose role it will be to explore this aspect. The simplest approach here is a five-step one:

1. The group of volunteers meets and establishes exactly what is needed (e.g. better student behaviour, improved results for boys).

2. The group consults and discusses the latest theories and thinking and identifies approaches and strategies that might work in your school.

3. Each volunteer tests one or more of these out at least three times in their own classroom.

4. The volunteers feed back their findings to each other, draw conclusions and plan a way forward for the whole school.

5. The group shares what they have discovered with the entire staff and make their recommendations for a whole-school approach.

■ To encourage problem sharing and collegial collaboration, prepare a 'wingman timetable' for display in the staffroom or electronically. This is simply a chart showing the days of the working week along with the lesson slots. On this timetable, staff are invited to highlight where they would appreciate support in a lesson – perhaps assistance with, or feedback on, a new technique they want to try. If another colleague is not teaching during that time slot and feels they can spare some time, they can turn up to assist the teacher-in-need.

STAFF-LED DEVELOPMENT

■ There is usually a wealth of expertise and ideas among a staff team, and we should make sure we tap into this potential for the purposes of CPD. Try setting up a training event where staff attend sessions on a carousel basis. Each designated classroom can host a different 'in-house presenter' who will share a useful concept or innovation with a small group. At a given signal, the groups move to the next classroom, and so on until every delegate has attended every session. This approach to CPD works especially well if each delegate is given a bag and collects a physical object from each presentation (in addition to the new ideas they will take away). The takeaway item might be an advice sheet, a USB containing resources, an ink stamp, a book or some other physical resource.

■ If a whole staff team is going to attend the same training event then it is useful to survey staff to find out what they would most like that training to focus on. You might ask them to submit their suggestions anonymously so that no one need feel nervous about divulging their development need publicly. Once you've collected the data, look for common threads and ensure that this valuable information is used when determining the topics of whole-school INSETs.

A DIALOGUE BETWEEN STAFF

■ Start a staff 'book club' where interested parties read and discuss texts related to teaching. Staff can meet to exchange views about the ideas presented by the book, as well as feed back on techniques they have trialled in their own lessons. Colleagues can be encouraged to annotate the books (perhaps with sticky notes), highlighting interesting passages and reporting on personal experiences. These annotated copies can then be left in the staffroom for other teachers to peruse.

■ When staff need to come together to discuss an important issue, it is often only the most vocal or confident members of the team who get their voices heard. Try suggesting that the debate takes place through the medium of writing: provide large sheets of paper on which staff can 'discuss' their views and argue or agree with other people's statements. Invite staff to move around the room adding their thoughts and responses to the debate emerging on each sheet of paper. This process can be done anonymously and captures the opinion of every member of staff. It also allows colleagues to enter into a dialogue with people they might not normally question or respond to in a traditional whole-staff discussion.

■ Set up a 'solution share' board (either physically or electronically) where teachers can post teaching and learning problems they currently have (e.g. 'I can't get any of the girls in my Year 10 class to contribute to class discussion'). Colleagues are then invited to review this board on a regular basis and respond with their own tried and tested practical solutions. All of this can be done anonymously if you wish. It is a powerful way to encourage teachers to share their experiences and talk about pedagogy. A designated area for sharing problems and solutions sends a clear, reassuring message to staff – that we all encounter roadblocks. Members of the SLT who teach may be the best people to set this ball rolling!

SHARING LESSONS

▪ Encourage your colleagues to have their lessons filmed. (Remember, it is possible to film the learning and the impact of the teaching without even getting the teacher in the frame!) Reviewing oneself on film can be a remarkably insightful experience. Videos of lessons can be used in a variety of different ways. For example:

> To demonstrate individual techniques via a video-clip TeachMeet.

> To evaluate lessons with colleagues and co-plan subsequent lessons.

> To connect with other schools and exchange ideas.

> To share clips with students and ask them to scrutinise their own learning behaviours.

> To create a bank of lessons for staff to view online (each video can be accompanied by the planning and peer feedback).

> To advertise to parents.

> To demonstrate (and celebrate!) good practice without the observation seeming like a judgemental process.

> To enable close scrutiny of one's own practice so that precise elements of classroom practice can be deliberately targeted and enhanced.

■ Find colleagues who are brave enough to have video clips of their teaching analysed by peers, and set up a CPD cinema event. Invite staff to view and discuss the clips using non-judgemental language. You might like to provide the audience with popcorn and a list of questions which will ensure they are analytical rather than evaluative in their approach. Examples of useful questions include:

> Who is working harder – the pupils or the teacher?

> What new learning occurs?

> How does the teacher engage the learners?

> What do you notice about the teacher's/pupils' questions?

> How does the teacher get feedback about understanding?

> What do you notice about the feedback the teacher gives?

SUE COWLEY is a writer, presenter and teacher, and the author of 30 books on education. Her bestseller, *Getting the Buggers to Behave* (2014), has been translated into ten languages and is a set text on teacher education courses. She has written for numerous educational publications, including *TES*, *Teach Primary* and *Nursery World*. She has also appeared as an expert witness on behaviour before the House of Commons Education Select Committee. After training as a primary teacher, Sue taught English and drama in secondary schools in the UK and overseas. She works internationally as a teacher trainer and she has helped to run her local preschool for the last eight years. Her websites are www.suecowley.co.uk, www.roadschooldiary.co.uk and www.celebrate-writing.co.uk. Her blog is at www.suecowley.wordpress.com.

CHAPTER 4

CHANGE YOUR TEACHING, NOT YOUR LEARNERS

SUE COWLEY

If we want children to learn, they need to feel *engaged* with what they are learning, and *motivated* to learn it. These two facets of good teaching often cause confusion: some feel this is the same as saying teachers must make their lessons 'fun'. But that is a misreading of what is meant by these terms. You can feel fully engaged with something that you find difficult, if you see the purpose in what you are doing. You can feel highly motivated to struggle on with something hard, if you envisage a positive end result. Learning is often jolly hard work, and not much fun at all, but part of our job as teachers is to help children to stick at it.

There are many ways that a teacher can help students to feel motivated and engaged. (My book, *Getting the Buggers to Behave*, has a chapter on 'teaching for good behaviour'.) Often, it is about the relationship you have with your students: if they respect and want to please you, they are more likely to work well. If you have a passion for learning, and for the subjects you teach, this comes across in everything you do. You can find ways to make learning feel relevant and purposeful to your children – for instance, by using topical events or interesting resources. You can use targets and adapt the pace of the lesson to help the children maintain focus. You can tell stories, crack jokes, incorporate anecdotes and do a million other things to make the children *want* to learn what you need to teach.

There are many things in teaching that we can't change; the systems, the managers, the inspectors, the particular children we are given to teach. But there is one thing that we *can* change, one thing over which we *do* have control, and that is how we decide to teach. Yes, students have a responsibility to engage with lessons and work hard, but we can't do much about it if they refuse (apart from punishing them, which is counterproductive). Instead of focusing on what your students need to change about themselves, take control of your teaching and decide what you need to change about yourself. Be responsive, adaptable, creative and flexible. Think about what works for you as a learner, and then apply that to your kids.

FURTHER READING

Cowley, Sue (2014). *Getting the Buggers to Behave* (London: Bloomsbury).

Cowley, Sue (2017). *The Artful Educator: Creative, Imaginative and Innovative Approaches to Teaching* (Carmarthen: Crown House Publishing).

www.suecowley.co.uk

PRACTICAL STRATEGIES

Sue Cowley summarises some vital ingredients for effectively engaging learners. Try the following strategies for exploring her ideas further.

ENVISAGING A POSITIVE END RESULT

- Set up a routine whereby learners are required to predict their mark or grade (or summative comment) and record it before they attempt an assignment. Psychologically, this works well for keeping learners challenged and working at their highest capacity for the duration of a task.

- In addition to helping learners to set targets for the content and quality of their work, it can also help to keep them engaged by motivating them to beat quantity and time records. As you are circulating during independent work, agree with learners the aspirational times by which they will complete a stage of the task and note these down. Revisit the learners at exactly the agreed times to reinforce the challenge and celebrate their breakthroughs.

SEEING THE PURPOSE IN WHAT YOU ARE DOING

■ Give a task a sense of authentic meaning by making its purpose be to help other people. When learners need to express their understanding about a topic, ask them to produce a 'how to' video. These are now ubiquitous in modern culture and exist on YouTube for just about every skill imaginable, so there are plenty of examples you can use to illustrate the format. Using the immediately accessible medium of the moving image can be an instant motivator for pupils who will recognise the potential value of what they are producing for their audience.

■ Present learners with a genuine mystery to solve. This could be on a small scale (e.g. cracking a code or identifying a missing link) or a large – even whole-school – scale (e.g. an unidentified vehicle or container mysteriously appearing in the playground). Consider getting other colleagues and their classes involved in the intrigue. You might like to release information or clues in carefully spaced stages to keep learners fully captivated and engaged.

MAKING PUPILS WANT TO LEARN WHAT YOU NEED TO TEACH

As Sue Cowley points out, engagement will arise naturally out of challenge, so creating a scenario where the task is so enticing that there is simply no choice but to be involved will ensure that even the most reluctant pupils are drawn in to accept the missions we offer them.

■ Pupils can be newly motivated to explore ideas in writing simply by offering them novel surfaces on which to transcribe. Different canvases appeal to different learners. Try pinning up banquet roll to allow writing on walls or providing paper tablecloths to enable writing on desks. Liquid chalk pens can be used for writing on windows. The youngest learners can experiment with letter formation in sand, shaving foam or by chalking on pavements.

■ Ask learners to bring in one item from inside (or outside!) their home that relates in some way to the topic being studied. The link could be an obvious or a tenuous one. Display these items on a table and ask the class to peruse the objects, sharing their own theories for why each item is relevant. Learners can subsequently compare their own reasoning with that of each item's donor. At the end of a topic, when pupils can apply new learning to the display, they may well be able to point out brand new connections.

▨ Immerse your class in the topic they are studying by creating a bespoke environment in your classroom. You could achieve this by creating clever displays, rearranging furniture, playing pertinent music or sounds, or perhaps by exposing the class to a relevant odour. Try sourcing appropriate costumes or even providing food that relates to the topic being studied.

▨ Use unexpected resources to open up new creative possibilities for exploring a topic or skill. For example:

  ⟩ When pupils are working in small groups or pairs, place stopwatches or egg timers on each table to generate a sense of urgency and encourage unwavering focus. Keeping pupils very conscious of their use of time is a great way to boost engagement and motivation. Off-task behaviour often occurs when pupils do not feel under pressure to produce a specified level of work within a designated timeframe.

  ⟩ Write on wooden clothes pegs and use these to categorise items, quotes, examples, etc. They can be used to explore links between concepts, creatures, events or numbers. With some accompanying washing line you can also help pupils to consider the hierarchy of ideas and physically explore chronological order, order of preference or the order of steps to be taken in a task. Pupils could even create a progress display as the scheme of work unfolds, pegging up key points and adding suggestions and questions to an ever growing 'line of learning'.

> Use an inflatable ball to introduce the rule that 'catchers must contribute'. You could pass this around during question and answer sessions, use it to explore sequencing or simply encourage learners to build on each other's ideas. Try attaching colour-coded sticky note questions to it or allow learners to affix their own questions to it as it is circulated.

CHAPTER 5

THE ASSUMPTION OF EXCELLENCE

RICHARD GERVER

Award-winning former teacher and head teacher RICHARD GERVER works in education globally and is recognised as one of its most significant voices. His first book, *Creating Tomorrow's Schools Today* (now in its second edition), has become a seminal text around the world for those engaged in the transformation of education. He has taken his experience of leading a team to transform the fortunes of a failing school and uses it to explore the wider issues of motivation, leadership, human potential and success in many fields, including working in elite sport, high performing businesses and the music industry. He is the proud recipient of an honorary doctorate in education from the University of Derby.

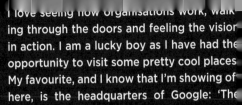

I love seeing how organisations work, walking through the doors and feeling the vision in action. I am a lucky boy as I have had the opportunity to visit some pretty cool places. My favourite, and I know that I'm showing off here, is the headquarters of Google: 'The Googleplex' in California. From the minute you arrive, you can't help being struck by the sheer energy and dynamic of the place; amazing people doing incredible things.

Of course, this vibe is no accident. When you ask around, what you realise is that the positive philosophy is built on the concept that I call, 'the assumption of excellence'. Google consider their staff to be the best of the best: highly skilled, intelligent and creative people. They are not 'managed' because the belief is that all 'Googlers' will excel; there is only intervention if people, for whatever reason, don't live up to that. This creates a culture of very high expectation but complete buy-in; people feel trusted and empowered, they feel free to create, collaborate and innovate and, most importantly, they believe that what they are doing is of real value.

Sometimes I fear that education policy and systems are designed from the opposing view – an assumption of incompetence. Political thinking would have us believe that teachers will only do their best if they are managed and pressured into doing so and that pupils are intrinsically lazy and therefore need managing, at times micromanaging, in order to succeed.

I passionately believe that as teachers and school leaders we should trust in our profession and our children more. We should audit our thinking and practice and build a culture that shouts about an assumption of excellence.

FURTHER READING

Gerver, Richard (2013). *Change: Learn to Love It, Learn to Lead It* (London: Penguin).

Gerver, Richard (2014). *Creating Tomorrow's Schools Today: Education – Our Children – Their Futures,* 2nd edn (London: Bloomsbury Education).

Gerver, Richard (2016). *Simple Thinking: How to Remove Complexity from Life and Work* (London: Wiley).

Robinson, Ken and Aronica, Lou (2015). *Creative Schools: Revolutionizing Education from the Ground Up* (London: Allen Lane).

PRACTICAL STRATEGIES

Too often in schools both staff and students can be plagued with fears around underachievement and not being 'good enough'. Richard Gerver's piece raises a significant question: how much of that is a product of our own discourse and monitoring systems? Are we operating from a position of target-meeting and preventing underperformance rather than creating a belief that excellence is not only attainable but the norm? Try some of these strategies to help foster a culture of empowerment and excellence rather than working from a deficit model.

TRUSTING AND EMPOWERING TEACHERS

- When it comes to teaching, work from an abundance model rather than a deficit one. Find out what each of your colleagues feels to be the strongest aspect of their teaching – the area where they feel they could most lend support and advice to others. Make a directory of staff and their areas of expertise. This will form a compendium that colleagues can consult when they are struggling with a particular aspect of their job or when the observation process identifies a specific area for development. Who could someone go to if they wanted help with differentiation? Behaviour management? Displays? Talking to parents? Writing reports? Giving effective feedback?

Questioning? The list you compile should be easily accessible, but it doesn't need to be displayed in a high profile place if you think it might embarrass your most modest colleagues. Consider keeping it as an electronic document that can be accessed discreetly when needed.

- Opportunities can be created for staff to contribute to school development by inviting them to put together bids or plans for moving the school forward in identified areas for improvement. The bids may include physical or e-learning resources, collaboration opportunities, requests for time and/or consideration of challenges/roadblocks in deploying their ideas and how to overcome them. Empowering staff to consider and share their thoughts and ideas about what will move the school forward shifts the thinking from top-down management into a more collaborative exercise. School leaders may also gain an awareness of strategies, resources and approaches from beyond the knowledge and experience of their core leadership team.

- As an occasional alternative to lesson observation, class teachers might like to prepare a self-reflection on a lesson (or series of lessons) that they will share with their line manager or a member of the SLT. Staff can explain the content of the lesson along with their own observations about what went well, scrutiny of student work that came about as a result of the lesson(s), what could have been improved and what teaching strategies or learning behaviours they may wish to develop as a result of the self-scrutiny. Asking teachers to reflect on their own practice and self-identify ways to move forward demonstrates a trust in their professional judgement and calls upon a greater sense of agency in professional development. It can also facilitate more meaningful conversations about teaching and learning and opportunities for sharing best practice.

TRUSTING AND EMPOWERING LEARNERS

■ Allow your learners to play an integral part in reporting on their progress and attainment – a process in which learners often feel disempowered and without agency. For written reports home, make it standard practice that learners include a personal statement about their successes and areas for development in the given reporting period. Ask them to comment on what their favourite units of study or assignments have been, to reflect on what aspects of their learning have been most challenging or where they would welcome additional challenge, and perhaps to comment on how they have involved themselves in extra-curricular opportunities in the school. Inviting students to have an element of ownership about what is being communicated to their parents and carers about their school life can be a great way to inspire them to ensure that there are high quality things to report!

■ Similarly, for parent–teacher meetings ask learners to create a plan for what they want their class teacher to discuss with their parents. The first time you ask students in your class for this, you will be met almost universally with the response, 'I don't know', because our learners are not typically consulted or perhaps are not trusted to share the 'right' information. Beginning parent–teacher meetings with an agenda of the learner's own priorities or thoughts on their learning draws the conversation more accurately back to what it should be: a three-way conversation about how to be the best learner possible.

■ Encourage reflection from learners about the ways they have involved themselves positively in a particular learning activity. Rather than waiting to be praised by a teacher or other adult in the classroom, establish a routine of learners spotting their own excellent contributions! You could encourage students to think about what the best question they asked that day was or the idea they shared that they were most proud of. You could ask them to reflect on ways that they supported their peers or on the strategies they used to help themselves get over being stuck or to up-level their work, rather than waiting for a teacher or peer to help them do it. Students so often rely on teachers to praise them and give them reasons to feel good about their learning. In order to empower students and perpetuate excellence we need our learners to be able to see these contributions for themselves as well.

ANDY COPE describes himself as a qualified teacher, author, happiness expert and learning junkie. He has spent the last ten years studying positive psychology, happiness and flourishing, culminating in a Loughborough University PhD thesis. His research feeds into a training course called 'The Art of Being Brilliant' which has been delivered to rave reviews all over the world.

Andy is also a bestselling author. He has co-authored the Art of Being Brilliant series for Crown House Publishing, which is aimed at teachers, as well as *The Art of Being Brilliant* (2010), *Be Brilliant Every Day* (2014) and *The Art of Being a Brilliant Teenager* (2014). He also moonlights as a children's author: *Spy Dog* (2005) won a Red House children's book award and the series has sold in excess of a million copies worldwide.

CHAPTER 6

SEX ON A SCHOOL NIGHT?

ANDY COPE

The average human lifespan is 4,000 weeks. If you announce that statistic to Year 3s they leap around, punching the air: 'Woo-hoo! Thanks for telling us, Andy. That's like ... forever!' But if you announce it to an adult audience there is less punching of the air and more of a collective gulp. The chances are your 4,000 weeks are zipping by in a blur.

As a teacher, there's a high probability of you being in a near-permanent state of physical and emotional exhaustion. Can you remember the last time you had sex on a school night? *Exactly!* You have a to-do list that's longer than both arms. Let me guess, you haven't got enough hours in the day to tick everything on that list? I appreciate that this causes you some angst, but my 300 words here are about something much bigger. Running alongside your to-do list is what I call your to-be list. And, in teaching, your to-be list is *everything*, because it dares you to point the finger back at yourself and ask, 'Who am I being while I'm doing my job?'

Am I being worn out by a wet break and an impending Ofsted visit? Or am I being radiant, positive, energetic and full of passion? Here's the spooky bit: by focusing on your to-be list, you are going to be more optimistic, creative, energetic, happy and, in a bizarre twist of quantum psychology, you will get more things ticked off your to-do list.

There's no denying that it takes a modicum of effort and practice to be your best self. Mediocrity is so tempting and easy. But my message is simple: the effort is well worthwhile. While focusing on your to-be list will not guarantee sex on a school night, it will massively improve your odds of having an all-round brilliant life.

FURTHER READING

Cope, Andy (2017). *Happiness: Your Route Map to Inner Joy* (London: John Murray Learning).

Cope, Andy and Bradley, Amy (2016). *The Little Book of Emotional Intelligence: How to Flourish in a Crazy World* (London: John Murray Learning).

Cope, Andy and Whittaker, Andy (2012). *The Art of Being Brilliant: Transform Your Life by Doing What Works for You* (Oxford: Capstone Publishing).

www.artofbrilliance.co.uk

PRACTICAL STRATEGIES

Andy Cope's suggestion that happy teachers make great teachers is an idea that is often echoed by learners when they are asked to describe their favourite educators. Conveying our own engagement in the topic we're teaching plays an important part in motivating our pupils. But how do we stay in touch with our optimism and enthusiasm in a profession that is often described as one of the most demanding? Try the following practical ways to keep your to-be list at the forefront of your daily teaching.

BEING RADIANT, POSITIVE, ENERGETIC AND FULL OF PASSION

- Take a good look at the colleagues you are spending most time with – do they inspire you? Make an effort to keep company with the people who are passionate about this profession: the ones who will elevate your own dedication and enthusiasm. Avoid spending unnecessary time with those colleagues who constantly emphasise the difficulties and disadvantages of teaching.

- Learners respond best when their teacher communicates an eagerness to teach. Convey your enthusiasm for your subject clearly through facial expressions and tone of voice. Radiate excitement when you introduce a new topic and your keenness will be contagious.

■ Set up a process that encourages colleagues to appreciate one another. One way of doing this could be a 'note of appreciation' form that staff are encouraged to send to each other, detailing the support they're thankful for. These can be duplicated for the line managers of the person being thanked and ultimately placed into staff files as a record of the many ways individuals contribute to the wider school life. Alternatively, try creating a staffroom display or 'appreciation wall' on which teachers, managers and support staff can publicly acknowledge and thank their colleagues for help given.

■ Emphasise the importance of being creative and daring by making 'Caution: risk in progress' signs for teachers to pin on their classroom doors when they are attempting something new. This will help to develop an ethos in which innovation and professional development are genuinely held in high esteem.

BEING YOUR BEST SELF

■ Foster an ethos of resource sharing across your team. Whenever you create something that works well in your classroom, make a copy for anyone else who might find it useful. Set up an electronic folder or online forum where everyone is encouraged to share resources they make. Some people can be quite territorial about their resources, but persevere and colleagues will soon catch on to the time-saving benefits of this approach.

◼ Remember to spread your collegial care and support to non-teaching staff, such as IT technicians, caretakers and office staff. These people have the capacity to save you valuable time, and conveying your respect and gratitude whenever possible is extremely important. If you are lucky enough to have the support of a classroom assistant, be sure to take the time to regularly and explicitly acknowledge all the ways in which they make your day run more smoothly.

CHAPTER 7

ASKING QUESTIONS TO BUILD PARENTAL ENGAGEMENT

PROFESSOR BILL LUCAS

PROFESSOR BILL LUCAS is director of the Centre for Real-World Learning at the University of Winchester. An acknowledged thought-leader in education, Bill has been a school leader and the founder of two national educational charities. With Guy Claxton he created the Expansive Education Network for schools, the educational goals of which are reflected in their book, *Educating Ruby* (2015). As an author, often with Guy Claxton, he has written more than 40 widely translated books which have sold more than half a million copies, including *Help Your Child to Succeed* (with Alistair Smith, 2002) and, for the BBC, *Happy Families: How to Make One, How to Keep One* (with Stephen Briers, 2006). Bill is in demand across the world as a researcher, speaker and facilitator.

When I was CEO of the Campaign for Learning I wanted to find out what messages would turn people on (or back on) to learning. So we commissioned MORI to ask the public in a series of surveys. We tried out phrases like 'learn to earn', which worked quite well for those primarily motivated by money. But the one that was most powerful across all groups was 'discover your hidden talents'.

One of the key groups we wanted to engage was young single mothers, often of school age. They were a group much criticised in the press as being hapless and irresponsible. Our hunch was that even this group of apparent ne'er-do-wells could be turned on to learning and reintegrated into school or college. We were right, for even this group of accidental parents wanted their children to do well at school. In fact, they were very determined that their own children would do better than they had at school, and were willing, therefore, to focus on literacy, for example, so that they could help their child.

Asking good questions of your staff is especially important when engaging parents in their children's learning at school. The questions themselves invite possible courses of action. They provide a baseline. They build understanding. The same process, of course, needs to be undertaken with parents directly. Then it is a matter of making a plan, forming a team

QUESTIONS WHICH HELP

1. Are there clear, friendly signs throughout the school?

2. Where can parents/families meet?

3. Do we have a parent display area with notices changed on a daily basis?

4. How often do we tell parents what children will be learning and how they can help?

5. What information do we give parents about local informal learning opportunities?

6. When do we invite new parents to observe teaching at first hand?

7. Do we make contact with parents about children's progress at least once a month?

8. Is the school voicemail checked every hour and messages acted upon?

9. Do we run workshops on 'learning parenting', covering themes such as setting high aspirations, giving praise, keeping boundaries, sleep, healthy lifestyles and so on?

10. To what extent do we understand the key aspects of what makes a successful parental engagement strategy?

FURTHER READING

Claxton, Guy and Lucas, Bill (2015). *Educating Ruby: What Our Children Really Need to Learn* (Carmarthen: Crown House Publishing).

Lucas, Bill (2013). *Engaging Parents: Why and How* (London: SSAT).

PRACTICAL STRATEGIES

Bill Lucas' cogent focus here reminds us that effective engagement of parents is about creating opportunities for parents to be involved in the fabric of the school and having clear mechanisms for sharing information about how they can best play a part in their child's success. Lucas' questions form a wonderful starting point for reflecting on your own school's processes and identifying where parental engagement could be developed. The following practical ideas may help you fill some of your 'gaps'.

ENGAGING PARENTS WITHIN THE SCHOOL

- Organise a 'bring an adult to school' day. This type of event can provide an excellent forum to build links with significant adults in your students' lives and give those parents/carers/grandparents some insight into what learning looks like for the child on an average day. Knowing what the classroom routines feel like, seeing how their child interacts with their peers in the classroom or experiencing some of the different learning strategies that their child works with can really help them to understand how to support their child at home. To avoid the challenging logistics of accommodating 30 additional adults in your classroom at the same time, it can be useful to allocate several days where parents can sign up for a session or time slot.

- Host a 'parental surgery' once or twice an academic year to give parents or carers an opportunity to discuss any issues with class teachers or school leaders. The 'surgery' can be generic, where parents are welcome to come and ask questions/seek information about individual needs, or you could hold themed events, where you specify that there will be members of staff there to field questions on a specific topic, like supporting homework, encouraging reading for pleasure, supporting relationships with peers or learning through play.

- 'Come and see my best work' events are a great way for both the school and learners to showcase the excellent work that has been taking place across the school. Through these, each class or faculty has an opportunity to gather the best examples of the most exciting projects they have undertaken over the course of the academic year and showcase them for parents and carers. A gallery approach is effective, with students and parents able to peruse and admire classmates' work at their own pace. You might choose to have the displayed outcomes manned by a representative of the class so they can contextualise the work and field any questions that may arise. Performance pieces and videos make a wonderful addition as well.

ENGAGING PARENTS AT HOME

■ Homework can often be a contentious subject with both learners and parents; if homework is not 'engaged with' in a meaningful way it can very quickly become a time-wasting affair for all parties concerned. Offering parents clear guidance about how they can best support their child in the homework that is set can go a long way to ensuring that the vital encouragement from home is in place. This will look very different depending on the age of the learner and the subject or topic they are working on. Ask yourself what ideal support from home would look like and work backwards from there. Some of the core issues to consider include:

› How are you communicating the purpose of homework to parents? The purpose of the task may be to encourage dialogue about their learning at home, to prepare for exams, to extend or enrich classroom learning, to embed ideas that learners have encountered in the classroom, or a combination of all these things. The level or type of support parents provide may be very different depending on what the class teacher wants to achieve through the piece.

› How do parents support their child in homework where their own subject knowledge may be lacking? Can you direct them to helpful websites or resources that can bridge the knowledge gap?

> Do parents have any reference point for standards of presentation or quality/length/breadth of work so they can help their child to check their homework? This works best if it is linked to feedback/self-assessment practices that already take place in the classroom.

> How much time are learners expected to spend on a homework piece?

■ Any parent with a school-age child will tell you that it can be incredibly difficult to get their child talking about school. Share with your parents and carers some ideas about how to move beyond the good old 'How was school today?' question to ones that will elicit a more descriptive response than 'It was OK.' Some helpful tips on improving the dialogue include:

> Allow children to not talk about their day when they are first picked up/arrive home. Leaving them to put some mental space between their day and a conversation about it can improve the dialogue vastly.

> Wherever possible, ask questions specific to what you already know is occurring in their day. Are they studying a particular topic? Do they have an assessment that day? Are they working with a teacher

or peer that is out of the ordinary? Did they have an issue or problem that they needed to resolve?

> Share an interesting event from your own day to begin the conversation. Sometimes this can be just the thing to prompt them to talk about their own day!

■ Sometimes getting the conversation going can need a little push. These prompts can be good conversation starters:

> Tell me something you learned today that you didn't know before.

> What was the best question you asked today?

> What piece of work did you put the most effort into? Why?

> What was the most difficult task you were asked to do today?

> Who did you work with today?

> Tell me something good that happened today.

> Tell me something funny/weird that you heard in class.

■ Involve parents in some action research. After a teacher–parent meeting, or when reports or interim grades have been sent home, ask parents to set a target with their child related to their home–school relationship. It may be something as simple as getting up ten minutes earlier to avoid the before-school rush or something more curriculum based, like reading three non-fiction books this term. Ask parents to share their findings about the success of the target at an appropriate, mutually agreed juncture.

IAN GILBERT is an educational speaker, award-winning writer and editor, innovator, entrepreneur and a man who the *IB World* magazine named as one of its top 'educational visionaries'. In 1994 he established the unique educational network Independent Thinking, whose Associates and pioneering books have influenced teachers, school leaders and young people all across the globe. Ian has a unique perspective on education having lived and worked in the UK, the Middle East, South America, Asia and, now, the Netherlands. He is the author of titles including *Why Do I Need a Teacher When I've Got Google?* (2011) and the ever-popular Thunks books.

CHAPTER 8

THE B-WORD

IAN GILBERT

'We are boring the motivation out of our children. Disaffection means "to cause to lose affection or loyalty". We are the cause. We dis-affect children. We talk about motivation but we need to have a serious conversation about de-motivation.'

I wrote these words in 2008 in a report that we were commissioned to write on learner motivation for the since-demised Qualifications and Curriculum Authority, led by the still very active Mick Waters. It was a heady time of personal learning and thinking skills, every child mattering and the promise of a Rose Review that actually wanted primary children to enjoy their lessons.

Of course, that has all changed now.

The resurgence of 'traditional' teaching, championed by the Conservative government and its carefully selected and ubiquitous champions, has relegated children actually enjoying their lessons back down the list of priorities, behind test results, behaviour management, Ofsted and where we will end up on the PISA scores next time round. A successful school has become one measured only by what can be measured, what is being measured has become even narrower, and the mark of whether a particular teaching approach is effective or not is evaluated solely by its effect on academic progress gauged by test scores and exam results.[1]

It is a curious state of affairs that has been described as the 'state theory of learning'; that is to say: 'A highly regulated system in which performance can be measured quantitatively by test results. The attendant theory of motivation is that teachers and pupils will be driven to improve against the state determined performance targets' (Lauder, 2009: 200, quoted in Brown, 2015: 3).

In other words, education has become the process by which we get the largest amount of children through the narrowest of hoops in the most efficient manner.

By 'children' I mean 'data'.

And by 'efficient' I mean 'joyless, uninspiring and entirely utilitarian'.

Which brings us back to the 'B-word'.

When considering the role that boredom plays in our classrooms, there are some aspects to clarify first. Bad teaching is bad teaching, whichever end of the tiringly Manichaean 'trad vs. prog' debate it is on. In my many years going into classrooms, I have seen child-centred rubbish and I have seen teacher-led rubbish. And in my own children, going through various school

---

1 'Great teaching is defined as that which leads to improved student progress' (Coe et al., 2014: 2).

systems, I have seen a son as demotivated by being taught relentlessly from the front as my daughter was demotivated by not being taught enough.

What also needs highlighting is that the opposite of 'boring' isn't 'fun'. Engaging, rewarding, demanding, hard, challenging, taxing, absorbing, motivating – all those words are the opposite of boring.[2] As well as fun.

Perhaps the best way to explain what is needed for children to be learning at their best is to use a term from paediatric neuroscientist Dr Andrew Curran, when he describes the essential role that the neurotransmitter dopamine plays in learning and memory. What generates dopamine principally is 'reward and the anticipation of reward' (Curran, 2008: 79); that is to say, doing something that is *intrinsically rewarding to us* (which will be different things for different people) or knowing we are about to do something that is rewarding.

In other words, and in a 'best of the best' way, we know of at least seven factors that will help get children motivated in the classroom:

1. We offer them a variety of learning approaches.

2. We stretch them in a positive way.

3. We look like we like them.

---

2 In fact, in the research I mentioned earlier, it was the word 'practical' that kept coming through in our interviews with children, used as if it were the antonym of 'boring' for them.

4. We let them know that they are not their test results.

5. We pay attention to the things we do that demotivate motivated children (your teaching assistants will tell you what these are, as will the children themselves).

6. We remember that we are probably not the most interesting person in the world.

7. We look to engage them with active, interesting lessons more than we look to punish them for playing up in passive, boring ones.

If we know this, why are we not being encouraged to do more of it? To answer this we would do well to go to the research of Dr Ceri Brown in her insightful book *Educational Binds of Poverty*. In it she says: 'performative pedagogies, consistent with the demands of the state theory of learning, create passive and conforming learners', adding that such qualities 'are not the learning orientations required to be academically successful' (Brown, 2015: 28).

With the current focus on grades and the obedience needed to passively acquire them, we are in danger of generating learning at the expense of creating learners. Furthermore, as Dr Brown's research exposes, this is all the more the case with some of our most needy young people (Turner, 2017).

Rather than using our children to improve our data, we need to use the data at our disposal to improve our children, with the overriding target – far more important than the grades – being that we educate them to be happy, healthy and confident young people who get a genuine buzz from both the idea and the practice of learning. Now surely that's a far better B-word.

FURTHER READING

Brown, Ceri (2015). *Educational Binds of Poverty: The Lives of School Children* (Abingdon: Routledge).

Coe, Robert, Aloisi, Cesare, Higgins, Steve and Major, Lee Elliot (2014). *What Makes Great Teaching? Review of the Underpinning Research* (London: Sutton Trust). Available at: https://www.suttontrust.com/wp-content/uploads/2014/10/What-Makes-Great-Teaching-REPORT.pdf.

Curran, Andrew (2008). *The Little Book of Big Stuff About the Brain: The True Story of Your Amazing Brain* (Carmarthen: Crown House Publishing).

Gilbert, Ian (2007). *The Little Book of Thunks: 260 Questions to Make Your Brain Go Ouch!* (Carmarthen: Crown House Publishing).

Gilbert, Ian (2017). *The Compleat Thunks Book* (Carmarthen: Independent Thinking Press).

Lauder, Hugh (2009). Policy and Governance: Introduction. In Harry Daniels, Hugh Lauder and Jill Porter (eds), *Knowledge, Values and Educational Policy: A Critical Perspective*, Volume 2 (Critical Perspectives on Education) (Abingdon and New York: Routledge), pp. 199–201.

Turner, Camilla (2017). Number of poor students dropping out of university at highest level in five years, *The Telegraph* (29 June). Available at: http://www.telegraph.co.uk/news/2017/06/28/number-poor-students-dropping-university-highest-level-five/.

PRACTICAL STRATEGIES

Ian Gilbert challenges us to pay careful attention to the aspects of our education system and our programmed, automatic practice which may be undermining our conscious efforts to engage our learners. Below are suggestions for exploring some of the motivation 'factors' that he has listed.

STRETCH THEM IN A POSITIVE WAY

■ Generate excitement and ensure that each learner is stretched appropriately by presenting tasks as challenging 'missions' in 'Mission Impossible' envelopes. Create an enticing sense of urgency by specifying a time limit and displaying the countdown prominently. This strategy will also enable you to differentiate the level of challenge if necessary.

■ Add an extra element of challenge (and surprise) to the activity above by periodically throwing a spanner into proceedings. For example, 'The recipient of the vehicle you're designing has no arms', 'You must now revise your answer so it is conveyed in only three sentences', 'Soldiers have now blocked that exit, you must alter your plan of escape'.

■ Use Ian Gilbert's 'Thunks' to engage your learners in intelligent reasoning.[3] 'Thunks' are captivating questions that require a person to think deeply and laterally and can cause a learner to feel irresistibly caught up in intellectual, moral and philosophical rumination or discussion (e.g. 'If an animal could talk, would it still be OK to eat it?'). Any topic you are teaching can naturally throw up a Thunk, but you can find hundreds of examples in Ian's books, listed in the further reading section.

LOOK LIKE YOU LIKE THEM

■ Pick one learner each day/week who you will resolve to get to know better. Take the time to have a one-on-one discussion with this pupil and make a note of their interests, hobbies and perhaps even the date of their birthday. Find out what they want to become when they are older, what is important to them right now and if they offer information about their family background or important upcoming events at home, make a mental record of these things so you can subsequently enquire about them when appropriate.

■ Emphasise to your learners what you have in common with them. What mutual interests, hopes or fears do you share

---

3 Thunks® is a registered trademark of Independent Thinking Ltd.

with your class? Make a point of casually communicating these important points of collective experience as a natural part of relating to your class.

- Break down unhelpful them and us/teacher vs. students barriers in your lessons by actively participating in the learning experience. Rather than setting up an activity and then watching it unfold, try modelling what it looks like to be a good learner in this scenario by getting among the learners and joining in the activity.

- Create a book of positive observations about students in your class with a designated page for each learner. Pupils who crave attention often learn that they get noticed more easily when they are disengaged. Show your class that you notice the little things, such as acts of kindness, periods of focused independent working, a good question and so on. This strategy fosters a sense of mutual respect between teacher and learner, and you will find that the pupils love to look at this book and see the observations you've made about them.

THINGS WE DO THAT DEMOTIVATE MOTIVATED CHILDREN

■ Avoid beginning lessons with administration routines that turn the pupils off the learning from the outset. Copying down an objective can be a quick way to lose the natural anticipation and energy that pupils might automatically bring to a lesson. Instead, start lessons with a tantalising mystery or challenge that requires immediate attention and use this as a way to help learners engage with the learning objective instead.

■ Think carefully about the nature and purpose of the questions you are asking. If you are simply looking for one specific answer and the learners find themselves trying to guess what is in your head, they can quickly become frustrated and disinterested. Likewise, if you leave no time after your questions for learners to actually think about their response, they could easily become demotivated. Instead, ensure that your questions are designed to either ascertain what pupils are thinking or to cause them to think. Make a habit of pausing to allow thinking time during a question-and-answer session.

■ Rather than overloading learners with new information that they feel little personal connection to, encourage them to engage with the topic first by asking them to predict what will happen before a demonstration or guess the answer before it is revealed. You might even like to try covering up a section of a text or diagram and asking learners to use their knowledge and imagination to envisage what lies beneath.

THE MOST INTERESTING PERSON IN THE WORLD?

■ Engage your learners through the widely recognised power of storytelling. Stories connect our listeners to us and allow us to engage their emotions; they command people's attention and enable them to explore a subject from another angle. As the storyteller, it is easy to use proven techniques for audience engagement such as humour and voice variation. Try telling a story to share your own relevant experience or use a story to introduce a new topic or illuminate a concept. A good story can create suspense, intrigue and excitement in learning as well as allowing your pupils to relate to you as an authentic person. The building of anticipation and empathy that naturally accompanies storytelling will also help your listeners to personally invest in and care about what they are learning.

■ Many teachers find themselves repeating back or rephrasing everything their pupils contribute to class discussions. If this happens all the time it can cause learners to disengage whenever a classmate is speaking, so they don't have to listen to everything twice. Make a point of 'bouncing' from person to person during a class discussion. After each learner expresses his/her idea, turn to a different member of the class and ask them to comment on their classmate's contribution. This technique encourages learners to stay engaged and attentive. You might like to facilitate this 'bouncing' by using questions such as, 'What would you add to that answer?', 'What evidence would we need to contest that suggestion?' or even simply, 'What did she just say?'

SUSAN WALLACE is Emeritus Professor of Education at Nottingham Trent University. She previously worked for many years as a teacher and in a local authority advisory role for post-14 education. Her particular interest is in the behaviour and motivation of learners and, as well as academic research, she has written a number of popular books for teachers.

CHAPTER 9

BUILDING A RELATIONSHIP

PROFESSOR SUSAN WALLACE

The psychologist Carl Rogers (1902–1987) tells us that a positive relationship between learner and teacher is essential if effective learning is to take place. A positive relationship in this context doesn't mean that we have to act as though we're the pupils' best mate, but it does require us to build up a working relationship of mutual trust and respect. This isn't always easy. Learners of any age may come to us having had negative or even destructive experiences of being 'taught'. Their confidence in their own ability to learn may have been undermined, along with their enthusiasm for being in your – or anyone's – classroom. We always need to take into account, therefore, the possibility that a loss of motivation, leading to disengagement and – in some cases – non-compliant or confrontational behaviour, may have its roots in this fractured relationship.

As teachers, it is our responsibility to try to mend it, however resistant our learners appear to be. We can do this most effectively by modelling for our pupils ways of relating and interacting within the classroom that are positive, encouraging and respectful. This also means making pupils feel that we value them and the time we spend with them; that we are happy to be there, working with them; and that our enthusiasm for them and the subject we're teaching them is boundless.

This is a tall order, certainly – especially on a bad day. But it's a long-term strategy that's well worth persevering with.

FURTHER READING

Wallace, Susan (2013). *Managing Behaviour in Further and Adult Education: Achieving QLTS*, 3rd edn (London: Learning Matters/ SAGE).

Wallace, Susan (2017). *Motivating Unwilling Learners in Further Education: The Key to Improving Behaviour* (London: Bloomsbury).

PRACTICAL STRATEGIES

■ Make sure you know every learner's name and use it *every time* you speak to them. Use names at every opportunity. It emphasises that your relationship is with each individual and suggests that you don't view them as simply A. N. Pupil.

■ Smile as much as possible (or as much as is reasonable without appearing deranged) and look happy to be there. Recent research has shown that teachers who look 'cheerful' experience fewer incidents with learner disengagement.

■ Be approachable. If a pupil has 'switched off' because of a previous negative classroom experience, finding you scary will do nothing to remedy this.

■ Demonstrate a sense of humour – even if it sometimes means laughing at yourself. Pupils find it easier to relate to someone who's human.

■ Take every opportunity to talk to disengaged learners one to one. This may not be easy when you're rushed for time, but it does pay off.

ANDY GRIFFITH is the creator of the Outstanding Teaching Intervention (OTI) and is a director of MALIT Ltd. He has helped teachers and whole schools move up to Ofsted's outstanding grade by offering practical advice and getting teachers to try new ways of working with their students. Andy has won a national training award and has written and consulted for a number of organisations including the BBC and Comic Relief.

CHAPTER 10

FLOW

ANDY GRIFFITH

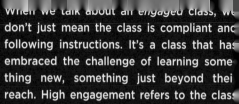

When we talk about an *engaged* class, we don't just mean the class is compliant and following instructions. It's a class that has embraced the challenge of learning something new, something just beyond their reach. High engagement refers to the class being absorbed in the challenge of their learning. By contrast low engagement is where you see learners nowhere near being absorbed. For me the terms engagement and challenge are synonymous. The engaged learner has accepted the challenge they have set themselves or have been set by their teacher. The challenge could be to think beyond their current level of understanding, to try something new or to reflect back on a piece of work and consider how it could be improved.

Because engagement and challenge are two sides of the same coin, I have been drawn to a simple yet elegant theory – the theory of flow. This theory is the work of Professor Mihaly Csikszentmihalyi (1990), who for many years has been the world's leading expert in the field of optimal performance. I referred to it extensively in the first book I wrote with Mark Burns, *Engaging Learners* (2012). The characteristics of being 'in flow' are that you completely lose yourself in the activity you're engaged in: 'Minutes become hours, hours become days. You become so focused and energised that distractions cannot enter your thoughts' (Griffith and Burns, 2012: 10). Such activity is highly pleasurable, and the good news is that it seems that everyone is capable of this state of flow across a vast range of experiences.

Flow occurs when high skill levels meet high challenge, as shown in the diagram on page 94. A careful look at the axes can help us to engineer high engagement in our classrooms. Consider the bottom axis first. We all appreciate that it is easier to teach a group of children or adults who hold a positive attitude to learning. They like learning, they even like thinking! When set a challenge they rise to it and take enjoyment from trying to work through the problem. It is also easier to teach highly skilled learners. Those learners who already have an established set of 'skills', such as being reflective, or speaking, reading and writing fluently and so on, are only going to be in one of two states according to the theory – either boredom or flow. They will attain flow if the teacher sets a challenge that the students believe they can achieve. However, pitch the challenge too low and these highly skilled and motivated learners will become bored. This is why it is so important to properly pre-assess learners before every topic.[1]

---

1 Interested in more about pre-assessment? Then visit www.malit.org.uk and follow the link to the Teaching Backwards Topic Planner. Here you will find a free topic planner that can be downloaded in different formats and a video tutorial. It explains where pre-assessment sits within the Teaching Backwards methodology.

Anxiety	Flow
Apathy	Boredom

LEARNING ATTITUDES AND SKILLS   High

Source: Griffith and Burns (2012: 1

ntrast, we may meet a class in September and mar
be low in terms of skills or attitude, or both. Accordir
kszentmihalyi's model, these learners are most likely
athetic, or when the teacher does try to challenge the
will become stressed. However, all of the students in th
are capable of achieving the state of flow. For this to har
their teacher will need to boost their skills and alter,

what the best teachers do. They use a variety of strategies to boost the attitudes of learners and develop the skills that will help them to work better with their teacher, with their class-mates and, perhaps most importantly, by themselves.

The theory of flow celebrates a state which one might call hap-piness. It is a place we go to challenge ourselves, where we enjoy our time on this planet fully absorbed in some kind of meaningful struggle. It can be hard for each person to attain, but like Csikszentmihalyi, I believe that everyone can attain this optimal level of engagement. It is something that I hope you, the reader of this chapter, experience in your personal and pro-fessional lives. If you are a teacher aspiring to get as many of your learners in flow as possible, it may help to think about the right conditions to create this. It will be different for each class you teach, but this useful theory can help you to help others experience this too. Wouldn't that be something?

FURTHER READING

Csikszentmihalyi, Mihaly (1990). *Flow: The Psychology of Optimal Experience* (New York: Harper and Row).

Griffith, Andy and Burns, Mark (2012). *Engaging Learners* (Carmarthen: Crown House Publishing).

Griffith, Andy and Burns, Mark (2014). *Teaching Backwards* (Carmarthen: Crown House Publishing).

PRACTICAL STRATEGIES

PRE-ASSESSMENT

■ The quickest way to disengage a learner is to teach them something they already know. Before you embark on any topic, find some time to pre-assess what each learner knows, understands and can do for the upcoming topic. It is advisable to do this a few weeks before to give you time to adjust your planning. Put another way, you either pre-assess the learners' starting points or you guess them. There are some simple pre-assessment techniques that take as little as five minutes. A cold task is a good example of this. A few weeks before an upcoming topic, set learners a cold task individually and in silence. This could take the form of a piece of writing, a mini test, an examination question, a comprehension of key terms or a diagram such as a concept map. The task should reflect something they will encounter in the upcoming topic; it may even be assessed within that topic. When you process the pre-assessments you might find that some learners have achieved 9 out of 10 in the test or demonstrated a high degree of fluency in the cold task. This informs you from the outset that these learners should be set a higher initial challenge.

LEVELLING UP

■ Ratings, scales or levels help us in many aspects of our lives. There are 'levels' for restaurants rated by the likes of the famous Michelin Guide. The more stars the restaurant has, the better quality dining experience you would expect. Similarly, martial arts move from a white belt up to a black belt and then new levels, or dans, after that. These scales help to inform us and give us information about what we have to do to attain a particular level. How about creating a set of levels for, or with, your class? At each level there can be a simple descriptor. Ensure that the top-level descriptors encourage students to think hard, work outside their comfort zone and so on. Make sure that the bottom descriptors articulate the behaviours that you don't want to see, such as not trying, not reflecting and so on.

■ Many teachers have realised the power of using metaphors with their class. When levelling up a habit, skill or attitude with your class, try combining the levels with a metaphor. For example, quality of food or even biscuits (who could forget comedian Peter Kay's sketch about the best biscuits to dunk in your tea?). Other examples might include computer game levels, football leagues, curry strengths, Olympic medals, animals or mobile phone types. The list is endless. Against your top level, such as 'gold medal', write a descriptor which requires absolute perfection. The description of the silver medal will need to be slightly less than perfect and so on. Ensure that there is a buy-in to the metaphor from the class. The top level should be something they aspire to and the bottom levels should be something they consider to be low quality or naff. Change the descriptors as necessary to ensure they always challenge learners.

DR DEBRA KIDD taught for 23 years in primary, secondary and higher education settings. She is the author of *Teaching: Notes from the Front Line* (2014) and *Becoming Mobius: The Complex Matter of Education* (2015); however, her latest project, *Uncharted Territories: Adventures in Learning* (2018), with Hywel Roberts is her favourite because it represents where her heart is – in the classroom.

Debra is the co-founder and organiser of Northern Rocks – one of the largest teaching and learning conferences in the UK. She also has a doctorate in education and believes more than anything else that the secret to great teaching is to 'make it matter'.

CHAPTER 11

MAKING IT MATTER

DR DEBRA KIDD

In our education ideology wars, the word 'engagement' has become somewhat tarnished. One prolific education blogger declared 'engagement does not exist'. Of course it does, but what we consider to be engagement too often becomes conflated with fun. And the two are not the same. An engaged mind is one that is captivated in a state of confusion – that 'on the edge' feeling when we feel we are grasping at something almost within our reach, a something worth stretching for. What makes this extra effort worthwhile is what we need to be thinking about in terms of building memorable learning experiences for children. Because in that space, learning takes place.

Governments would have us think that 'grit' is the key to learning. The capacity to defer gratification and build resilience – these sit at the heart of what politicians call 'character education'. But it is perfectly possible to be resilient, to be able to wait, to endure and to become Stalin or the Child Catcher in *Chitty Chitty Bang Bang*. These qualities in themselves do not make for a better world. And surely that's what the purpose of education should be?

Instead, we should be thinking about what makes effort worth making. For human beings, a sense of purpose is key. Daniel Pink's work on motivation shows that the opportunity to have autonomy over a process, to feel that it has value (beyond monetary gain) and that there is a chance of mastering th skills necessary, leads to a strong sense of motivation. And recent research from Durham University (2017) showed that dialogic experiences such as Philosophy for Children (P4C) resulted in gains, even in maths. Making time to build children's capacity to engage with challenging ideas and concepts, giving them a structure to build a vocabulary with which they can articulate those ideas, and imbuing the whole with a sense of moral urgency and purpose leads to highly effective learning. In doing this, we create the only mantra we really need as teachers: make it matter. If you do, they will learn.

FURTHER READING

Kidd, Debra (2014). *Teaching: Notes from the Front Line* (Carmarthen: Independent Thinking Press).

Kidd, Debra (2015). *Becoming Mobius: The Complex Matter of Education* (Carmarthen: Independent Thinking Press).

Pink, Daniel (2009). *Drive: The Surprising Truth About What Motivates Us* (New York: Riverhead).

Roberts, Hywel and Kidd, Debra (2018). *Uncharted Territories: Adventures in Learning* (Carmarthen: Independent Thinking Press).

Siddiqui, Nadia, Gorard, Stephen and See, Beng Huat (2017). Non-cognitive impacts of philosophy for children (Project Report) (Durham: School of Education, Durham University). Available at: http://dro.dur.ac.uk/20880/.

PRACTICAL STRATEGIES

Debra Kidd illuminates an important shift in discourse around the issue of engagement: that engaging learners is not about entertaining them, but rather about making them *want* to learn what you need to teach them and to give it the very best they are capable of. Engagement is not some 'progressive' idea or fad, it is a necessary part of getting the very best out of learners that we possibly can. Use the following ideas to help you consider how to make learning in your classroom really matter to your pupils.

BUILDING MEMORABLE LEARNING EXPERIENCES

- Consider, from your own experience as a learner, what makes learning memorable. As a self-reflective exercise, pinpoint three of the most significant learning experiences from your own life (these need not necessarily be from school!) and try to work out what it was about the experience that was so memorable. Were you working independently or with a team? How were you supported through the learning experience? What kind of guidance was provided? Did you have special resources at your disposal? Was the setting significant? What skills did you use/develop? How did you feel at the beginning/middle/

end of the learning experience? Why? Catalogue the conditions that made your memorable learning experiences significant to you and use that as a planning tool, or perhaps as a means to reflect on your own teaching. How often do these conditions appear in the lessons you deliver? Perhaps get several of your colleagues to undertake the same task and then compare your findings. This can be an excellent platform for shared project planning and collaboration.

■ Learning is always more memorable when there is an element of discovery, as opposed to simply following a set of instructions and completing a task. Where possible, and with appropriate scaffolding, allow your learners to 'discover' rather than follow. Let your learners know what it is you want them to learn and work together to plan how they might do it. You may wish to give them some guidance about the types of resources at their disposal, such as available e-resources (websites, video clips, online tutorials, etc.), books, magazines, journals, exemplar material, problem-solving opportunities, images, diagrams, films, guest speakers, field trips, teacher instruction and so on. You, of course, will be the one to make the final judgement call on the programme of instruction, but allowing your learners some input in the course of action can be an excellent means to ensure that you are engaging them in the resources and opportunities that most interest them.

■ Grab learners' attention with something showy and flashy to get their curiosity flowing. Share an image or quotation that will surprise, amuse or maybe even confuse them. Show them a collection of topic-related objects and have them wonder how they all connect. Create a shocking tabloid-style headline (or perhaps a series of headlines) to give them a clue about the core theme or idea they will be exploring. Choose a figure from popular culture that embodies the ethos, values, characteristics or properties of the topic you are sharing with the class and let them speculate on how their learning today will be just like Jon Snow/Mickey Mouse/Owen Farrell. Foster a sense of wondering in your students from the outset and the thirst for learning, and impulse to discover the answers to those questions, will follow.

MAKE IT MATTER

■ Learners want to know that they have agency and can make a difference. Create opportunities in your teaching to show how what they are learning can impact both those around them and the wider world. Do some research into charities or organisations that have direct links to the areas of study that you have planned for the academic year and contact them to see what sort of resources/links they may have available to schools. Look into local/regional/national competitions that may allow your students to demonstrate their aptitude and take their learning into the wider community.

■ Create teaching or demonstration opportunities for your students to work with younger learners in your own school. Use older learners to deliver assemblies to younger ones on behaviour expectations or school rules and systems. Skills such as reading, basic numeracy and revision or study strategies can also be fruitful situations to pair learners of different stages together. Buddy systems, where the youngest learners in the school are each assigned a learner from higher up the school to mentor them throughout the school year, can be a fantastic way to build more sustained and supportive relationships.

■ Try to include a variety of ways that your students' work can be publicised and their very best efforts celebrated in places beyond their own exercise books or folders. Classroom displays are the obvious place to share students' work in a more public way, but other ideas include uploading images or copies to a class web page or blog, creating a magazine or portfolio (print or electronic) to share with the head teacher or parents, inviting a 'guest teacher' to come and view or perhaps assess the fruits of their labours, or initiating a mutual 'show and tell' of their work with a parallel class or group within the school. When learners believe that their teacher is the only audience for their work, they frequently make it 'good enough'. When they know that it has a wider interested audience, the stakes for improving the quality of their work are raised!

CHAPTER 12

KILLING THE IDEA KILLS EDUCATION

CONRAD WOLFRAM

European co-founder/CEO of the Wolfram group of companies CONRAD WOLFRAM is also founder of Computer-Based Math, an organisation dedicated to a fundamental reform of maths education. The movement is now a worldwide force in re-engineering the STEM curriculum with early projects in Estonia, Sweden and Africa. For more information visit: www.conradwolfram.com, www.wolframalpha.com and www.computerbasedmath.org.

I'm often asked how teachers should improve (normally low) motivation for maths at school. My answer is simple: give them problems to solve that they might care about! Things like 'Am I normal?', 'Are girls better at maths?' or 'Are home football referees biased?' Not what's x in $x^2 + x + 1 = 0$.

Maths is one of the world's most successful problem-solving systems, but we need to start with a problem that we (or our students) actually want to solve, not an abstraction they don't care about – and worse still wouldn't even ever use.

Maths is so important in today's real world because computers allow us to apply it to far more complex, real problems than when humans had to do all the calculating. Yet in education we're stuck on simplistic and often meaningless-to-the-student questions because we insist that the humans, not the computers, do the calculating. Teachers need to ask the fuzzy questions (like the ones you get in life) and the students should be using the power of abstract maths formulations (however complex) and coding to get the answer with help from their computer. It's much more motivating being a first-rate problem-solver than a third-rate human computer failing to compete with a machine! It's what the students crucially need for their futures, and what society does too.

Of course, different students will find different problems interesting, so be as flexible as possible in what they can work on.

After all, what's so powerful about maths is how disparate problems can often be solved with the same toolset.

Confidence is also central – of the teacher to be outsmarted (isn't it great when that happens?) and of the students to ask if they don't get something or to try a 'crazy' idea. Killing the idea kills education.

FURTHER READING

Wolfram, Conrad (n.d.). Making the Case, *Computer-Based Math*. Available at: http://www.computerbasedmath.org/case-for-computer-based-math-education.html.

PRACTICAL STRATEGIES

Learners being disengaged or lacking motivation in their studies because they don't see the point is not a challenge unique to teachers of maths; Conrad Wolfram's message about making learning relevant and based in the real world is pertinent to teachers of all subjects. Getting learners to ask questions and solve problems is not only a great way to enhance engagement, it also helps them to develop one of the most important skills of successful learners.

SOMETHING THEY MIGHT CARE ABOUT

- Few things are more 'real life' to learners than their outside hobbies and interests. Poll your class about their favourite pastimes and activities outside of school and tell them that you are setting yourself the challenge of showing them how their interests and hobbies apply to your subject area. Create a class display that shows your findings: where do skateboards feature in history? How does maths underpin their preferred social media platform? How is geography significant in the television series they are currently binge watching? Illustrating these connections for them may be just the spark needed to draw them into their learning. Even better, try to integrate these connections into the units of work you are studying over the course of the year.

■ Apply this approach to your learners' future career aspirations. You may be able to surprise them with the ways that your subject, or even a specific unit of work, can tie into the vocations that interest them. You might wish to include some unusual career choices that may not have occurred to them – who knows what sorts of aspirations you may trigger!

CELEBRATE THE TOOLSET

■ Raise the profile of the knowledge, skills and understanding that learners have mastered in your class by constructing a 'toolbox' for them to access. This may be a classroom display, a shared folder on the school's network, a 'get un-stuck stop' in the classroom, a portfolio they can browse through or a class website. Collating the core concepts, formulas, theories, terminology and skills, and having the collection easily accessible, can provide a great boost to confidence. This toolbox can act both as a celebration of how far they've come and as a reference piece when choosing their route into a problem.

DIFFERENT STUDENTS WILL FIND DIFFERENT PROBLEMS INTERESTING

- When presenting learners with a problem-solving opportunity in the classroom, try providing an element of choice. The options should all test the same objective and require similar skills to solve, but by varying the wording, stimulus, approach or mode of presentation your learners will be able to engage with the question that most captures their interest, which is sure to improve motivation.

- To give learners true ownership over problem solving, and to illustrate genuine comprehension of a concept and its core principles, challenge your learners to create problems for their peers to solve or questions for them to answer. Give your learners some clear style models to follow and guidance on the content/skills they need to test and you will have an excellent opportunity for your learners to sit on both sides of the problem-solving experience.

PAUL DIX is a speaker, author and notorious teacher-wrangler in huge demand. He is Executive Director of Pivotal Education. As a teacher, leader and teacher trainer, Paul has been addressing the most difficult behaviour issues in the most challenging schools, referral units and colleges for the last 25 years. He has advised the Department for Education on teacher standards, given evidence to the Education Select Committee and worked extensively with the Ministry of Justice on behaviour and restraint in youth custody. Paul co-hosts the Pivotal Podcast, which provides free training to over 250,000 teachers worldwide every week.

CHAPTER 13

TOMBOLA THEORY

PAUL DIX

Everyone loves a tombola. The prizes are awful, yet we love a tombola. Even those who win the top prize (bath salts nestled in crêpe paper aboard a mock woven basket) are tempted to give it back: 'Let someone else have the chance to win that magnificent prize – my bathroom is heaving with retro bathing products.'

Is it the attraction of the spinning box, the lightly taped raffle tickets or the lone tin of Spam that draws us to the mighty tombola? No. But I have worked out what it is. It is not the money or the prizes, it is not the charitable giving or the winning. It is the delving, the dipping, the curiosity of the result. It is the feeling of control and the sensation of risk. We will part with our hard-earned cash to feel the unique sensation of a hand in a sea of tickets, searching out possibilities.

Working with teachers in a residential school for children who had been thrown out of every other school, I was asked to come up with an idea that would 'motivate our students to do extension tasks'. A seemingly tall order given that most of the learners struggled to even get started. I gave the teachers shoeboxes and we spent a happy hour together pouring on glue and glitter to create 'sparkly boxes'. We filled each box with ten-minute extension tasks and placed the boxes at the back of each classroom, labelled with different levels of difficulty.

In the first lesson these supposedly 'disengaged' and 'unteachable' children were running to the boxes. Within a week the teacher had to slow them down; the children were rushing through the work to try to get to the extension tasks. The desire to delve immediately played havoc with the desire to disrupt.

The boxes motivate and focus the learning. They inject some interest into the lesson. They appear to give the child power over what is being studied. And they are thoroughly satisfying and sparkly.

What is the curiosity that leads your students to go 'over and above'?

FURTHER READING

Dix, Paul (2017). *When the Adults Change, Everything Changes: Seismic Shifts in School Behaviour* (Carmarthen: Independent Thinking Press).

www.pivotaleducation.com

PRACTICAL STRATEGIES

After hearing the tombola theory ...

- A maths faculty created a huge advent-style calendar with windows that were opened at the end of the lesson. Each day the learners revealed either a small reward for the class (night off homework, first to lunch, extra story time, etc.) or a maths investigation to be done over the weekend. The teacher could decide each day if a window had been 'earned' and the learners loved the jeopardy.

- A business studies teacher, utterly fed up with learners arriving late, decided to give envelopes out to the first eight who arrived on time. In the envelopes were small jobs that she needed them to do during the lesson. Within a week she had dramatically improved punctuality. One of the learners reported, 'We usually take the long way round but we really want to get an envelope now.' The learners were 18 years old.

> ■ One English teacher went sparkly-box mad. At last count there were eight different sparkly boxes/ bags/hats/tubes/socks. There were opportunities to delve for those who finished early, those who helped others, those who arrived early and those who helped themselves get unstuck. The children loved the variety and the teacher had become skilled at using the mechanism not simply to reward but to support, to extend learning and to get feedback on her own teaching.

Paul Dix urges us to recognise how an element of jeopardy and anticipation can immediately engage any class. Here are a few more tombola ideas:

■ Prepare a bag of random objects from which each group of learners must draw at the end of a lesson. After careful discussion and lateral thinking each group must explain how their object could be linked – either literally or metaphorically – to the lesson's content.

■ Place the names of all the learners into a receptacle. At pertinent points in the lesson, a name is drawn and that pupil is required to provide a 30-second summary of what has just been learned or to share the part of their assignment of which they are most proud.

■ Tell the class that you have chosen three 'secret students' in the classroom. If those students exhibit certain desirable learning behaviours during the lesson, the entire class will receive an appropriate 'reward' at the end. You might like to stipulate specific behaviours such as 'asking good questions' or 'completing at least one side of work'. This technique makes all the learners hyper-vigilant of their own learning behaviours as well as eager to support their peers in remaining focused and engaged at all times. If you decide to reward the class at the end of a lesson, you can reveal the name of the three successful secret students so that those individuals can bask in the gratitude of their peers.

CHAPTER 14

THE 300-WAY LEARNING METHOD

JOHN DAVITT

JOHN DAVITT is a poet, speaker and digital toolmaker. He has worked extensively with teachers in schools in the UK, United States, China and Africa over the last 30 years, and he is committed to levelling the playing field regarding access to new learning opportunities. John is the author of the book *New Tools for Learning* (2008) on how to make the technology fit the learning need, and the *WordRoot* CD, an interactive guide to words and their etymology. He has recently developed The Learning Score, a visual tool that lets teachers map out and share learning intentions as a graphical event, rather like a music score. His latest project is the 300wayLearn method, bringing delight, choreography and constraint to the learning process.

Contact or book a workshop via www.davittlearning.net, johndavitt@mac.com or @johndavitt.

How do you do? A formal enquiry we could also apply to the classroom. If the learning happens mostly in the doing – and research into active learning suggests that it does (see Petty, 2017) – then how exactly is the doing done? What is the main form of doing in the classroom?

If I were honest about my early years as a teacher the answer was: listen to me, watch this, now write about it. Now, for many learners that type of progression in instruction (listen > watch > write) is a Bermuda Triangle – a place from which little learning emerges.

This led me on a journey to explore the many ways of doing, of showing what you know, of demonstrating understanding. Wherever possible I looked to the use of media other than writing, searching out areas where the student may have greater mastery, such as talking, acting or drawing. I ended up with a list of 300 ways to do – and built a generator to randomly produce them in the classroom.

The aim behind my process was to up the range (and difficulty) of the learning challenge and to move activity from afterthought to art form. The final part of the jigsaw for classroom use of the method was to build in group work and repetition.

It is easy to think that groups are just collections of individuals, but in reality they are turbocharged learning resources – if they are tutored and allowed to be so. Groups can manage (and require) more dramatic learning challenges than 'write about it'. 'Tell the story of the heart as a mini opera' is a delight to a group (once they get past the shock!) but would often lead to failure for an individual.

'REPETITION IS THE MOTHER OF MEMORY'

Marvin Minsky reportedly said, 'You don't understand anything until you learn it more than one way', so the final ingredient in the method is repetition. Once you have asked the students to show 'peristalsis as a dance', then ask them to do it as a 'postage stamp illustration'.

FURTHER READING

Petty, Geoff (2017). Improving Progress By Learning from the Best Research. In Isabella Wallace and Leah Kirkman (eds), *Progress* (Best of the Best) (Carmarthen: Crown House Publishing), pp. 20–29.

www.davittlearning.net/200ways11.html (a 200-ways-to-show-what-you-know demo)

www.davittlearning.net

PRACTICAL STRATEGIES

As John Davitt points out, asking pupils to demonstrate their understanding through writing is often the default approach for both classwork and homework, but this kind of repetition can lead to disengagement. If your objective is to discover what learners understand or remember, then you should not feel limited to capturing this information solely through the written word. The following strategies offer an alternative to traditional written tasks, allow you to differentiate the learning experience and, in some cases, give you slightly less writing to mark!

THE MANY WAYS OF SHOWING WHAT YOU KNOW

- Make use of John Davitt's 200-ways generator which randomly generates a format in which pupils must depict their knowledge about a topic. For example, a learner might be asked to convey the concept of osmosis as a five-act play, an album cover or a rap. You can access the generator at: www.davittlearning.net/200ways11.html.

- Consider getting pupils to *choose* the manner in which they demonstrate their learning. This can work especially well for homework. You might find it useful to present learners with a menu of choices – for example, 'Demonstrate your understanding via a speech/cartoon/ chart/podcast/model/short film.'

■ Instead of taking notes from their reading or summarising a text in writing, ask learners to transform key information in the text into a new format. Getting them to use modelling clay to tangibly represent the main points and then removing the original text and using only the models to make written notes is one way of showing learners the difference between copying and actually condensing and transforming information.

■ Send one volunteer out of the classroom. While they are out of earshot, establish a rule in the room to which all the remaining pupils must adhere. The rule will obviously be linked to what the pupils have been learning about. For example, if you have been teaching them about different poetic devices, you may want to test their understanding of one of the devices by setting a rule like: 'You must use alliteration somewhere in your answer.' When the volunteer re-enters the classroom, he/she must select classmates at random and ask general small-talk questions, such as 'What did you do last night?', 'What did you eat for breakfast?' and so on. The volunteer must listen carefully to classmates' answers and try to determine what the rule in the room might be.

- You could ask pupils to cleverly include as many key terms from a particular revision topic into their answer as possible. They might be asked to follow the customs of a particular country or historical era. They might have to answer as if they are a given fictional character or famous figure. Or perhaps they have to use a particular grammatical device or persuasive technique, or answer in a particular rhythm, or each consecutive answer must follow a given sequence. As well as intriguing them and engaging them in a very enjoyable learning experience, this activity requires that the pupils give an 'understanding performance' – a demonstration of how well they have understood and can communicate a concept.

PHIL BEADLE knows a bit about bringing creative projects to fruit. His self-described 'renaissance dilettantism' is best summed up by *Mojo* magazine's description of him as a 'burnished voice soul man and left wing educationalist'. As songwriter Philip Kane, his work has been described in *Uncut* magazine as having 'novelistic range and ambition' and in *Mojo* as having a 'rare ability to find romance in the dirt' along with 'bleakly literate lyricism'. He has won national awards for both teaching and broadcasting, was a columnist for the *Guardian* newspaper for nine years and has written for every British broadsheet newspaper, as well as the *Sydney Morning Herald*. Phil is also one of the most experienced, gifted and funniest public speakers in the UK.

CHAPTER 15

ENGAGEMENT IS NOT *AN* ISSUE, IT IS *THE* ISSUE

PHIL BEADLE

I've long held a theory that I've rarely been brave enough to share with anyone: that there are two entirely different versions of teaching in British education, and they are not the same job at all. There's teaching in London and there's teaching anywhere else. My many travels have yet to convince me I'm wrong about this.

There are some very good schools in London, so I've heard, but with a single notable exception, it's never been my good fortune to teach in one. It matters not how well you've taught in previous schools when you are on your first or second week of duty in a London comp; few children are remotely interested in anything other than stealing your status and making you go away sharpish. I've had second-lesson gambits where children have entered the class openly declaiming, 'Not this idiot again.' On being informed that, 'You ain't teaching us anything' and in response, going back to the objectives to point out exactly what he had, in fact, learned, I have been further informed, 's entitled to my own opinion.' I've been called 'mad' regularly – by management as well as kids – and been in receipt of the sublime paradox of 'F*** off, sir' more times than I've had hot dinners. Behaviour in London schools is special, and in the least functional of these, rejection of learning can be absolute.

have never encountered any of this behaviour outside of London. When working with a group of students in Birmingham, Manchester, Newcastle or Scunthorpe, I'll be routinely and ruefully warned that a particular subset of students are 'completely intractable', only to find them lying on their backs waiting for their tummies to be scratched within about 15 seconds of meeting them.

This has caused me to wonder how far the current debate about engagement is affected by the environments in which the contributors to such debates teach. There is a modish view that any focus on engagement is almost anti-education, and that such a focus automatically ensures that you spend your whole teaching life constructing finger puppets of the three witches when you should be analysing Shakespeare's language. It seems to me, and I may be wrong, that this is a view held by people who teach in Dorchester, and that had they ever been in receipt of the full tsunami of the uncontrollable class who reject education, who reject the imposition of it from an outsider, and who will unleash the full genius of their hatred upon you if you seek to do anything other than let them stay in the chaos they inhabit, then they would think otherwise.

There are certain environments – specifically in London – in which engagement is not *an* issue, it is *the* issue. And the finger puppets are a useful bridge into the text, a way of making them tolerate your presence in front of them for just long enough that you might sneak some education in to let them know what it tastes like, so they might acquire an appetite for it. I understand the argument against engagement for engagement's sake, but it depresses me, as do its progenitors; as much as I am fairly sure their lessons depress their students. And I challenge them to come and take their falteringly inaccurate line-by-line analysis to a failing school in inner city London, and then, after several visits to a grief counsellor, come and tell an inner city London teacher that engaging students isn't important.

FURTHER READING

Beadle, Phil (2010). *How to Teach* (Carmarthen: Crown House Publishing).

Beadle, Phil (2011). *Dancing About Architecture: A Little Book of Creativity* (Carmarthen: Crown House Publishing).

Beadle, Phil (2017). *Rules for Mavericks: A Manifesto for Dissident Creatives* (Carmarthen: Crown House Publishing).

PRACTICAL STRATEGIES

Phil Beadle invites us here to put away our pedagogical snobbery, get over our purist attitudes about modes of delivering learning and get real about the people we teach. Not all of our learners are willing or biddable, and the lengths we go to in order to engage them in the learning experience are not frivolous or time-wasting but rather a display of our skill, insight and determination to make learning possible.

LET THEM KNOW WHAT IT TASTES LIKE

For some of our toughest customers, the way we present the learning, rather than the actual topic itself, can be the most significant deciding factor over whether they allow the information in or not. Being innovative in the way the information is presented or consolidated is not about 'entertaining' or sugarcoating the learning process, but rather a means of ensuring that learners are willing and able to do what comes next. Consider the following when looking to vary your mode of delivery.

■ Give learners the motivation to complete a complex task in small groups by breaking it into sections and releasing instructions in stages. Pupils will experience a sense of urgency and competition as they race to complete a stage. They must then send their 'runner' to you to gain your approval so they can secretly receive the next instruction, and so on. Each group is competing to be the first to successfully complete the whole task. Learners will quickly realise that they can't sacrifice quality for speed because if you are not satisfied with what a runner shows/tells you, they will be sent back to improve the work. This spirited strategy can be used to give even the driest topic an irresistible feel.

■ Put yourself in the role of 'interviewee' to bring important concepts about your current unit of study to life. Here, the teacher takes on a role and is questioned by the pupils about background, behaviour and motivation. For reluctant learners, having to be the interviewee themselves can be an anxiety-inducing situation that can quickly produce non-compliance. Allowing them to take on the role of questioner, however, can be an effective way to give your learners a sense of control. Rather than being the ones questioned and needing to recall or apply information, they get the opportunity to put you on the spot and make you illuminate the most important elements of their learning through the use of great questions. It can be an excellent way to bring humour into your lesson and can create very memorable delivery of content. This type of strategy need not be saved just for exploring fictional characters. You might take on the role of a transnational corporation, a disease, a drug, a president, a piece of equipment, a plant cell and so on. Give your learners some stem questions to model the kinds of questions that will best get the conversation flowing and then encourage them to begin devising questions of their own.

■ Bring some pace and excitement into consolidating the day's learning by challenging learners to create a super-speedy 'action replay' of the most important ideas that have emerged in that lesson. Set a time limit of no more than 90 seconds for the replay and arm your learners with strategies to help convey information in as brief a format as possible: using flash cards or mini-whiteboards to share key vocabulary and concepts; sharing widely understood abbreviations or acronyms; creating mnemonic devices to make crucial ideas or processes memorable; short, sharp sentences; images and diagrams that illuminate key ideas; movement and hand gestures to convey meaning; and, of course, speaking very, very quickly! Recording the action replay can provide an amusing recap of the learning to be used in future lessons as well.

■ Unite your class and instil a sense of competition by setting up a 'beat the teacher' challenge. Ask each learner in the class to prepare one question linked to your topic that they think you won't know the answer to, while you prepare an equal number of questions that represent information they have encountered in class. Take it in turns asking the class a question (to which they all reveal answers simultaneously with mini-whiteboards) and then allowing them to ask you a question from their challenge bank. The class earns a point each time they stump you, and you earn a point each time you ask a question that more than five people get wrong.

CHAPTER 16

USING DISCUSSION TO REFINE, ORDER AND ARTICULATE THINKING

MIKE GERSHON

MIKE GERSHON is the author of more than 80 books and guides covering different areas of teaching and learning. His online teaching resources have been viewed and downloaded more than 3.5 million times by teachers in over 180 countries and territories. Mike has written a number of bestsellers on topics such as differentiation, questioning, growth mindsets and assessment for learning. You can find out more, and train with Mike online, at www.mikegershon.com and www. gershongrowthmindsets.com.

Speech is a natural function of the human body. Writing is a technology. The former arises from our biological inheritance and the latter is a cultural product passed down through (usually) formalised education. For this reason, nearly all students are likely to be better speakers than writers.

Therefore, we can help students to experience success, and engage with our lessons and the topics we teach, by making use of discussion activities. For example, we might precede writing tasks with paired or group discussion. Or we might begin a lesson by posing a series of challenging questions which students first discuss in pairs before we lead a whole-class discussion.

Speaking and listening also gives students an opportunity to refine, order and articulate their thinking before capturing it in writing. Speech is ephemeral. If we make a mistake it slips away to nothing, and we can quickly edit and improve what we intended to say.

It follows that, by using discussion activities as a precursor to writing, we can help students to break up the cognitive load. First they refine, order and articulate their thoughts – within the safe, trial-and-error space of discussion. Then they commit these thoughts to paper – now being able to focus their full attention on the act of writing (as opposed to dividing their focus between deciding what they want to write and working

Discussion engages students because it gives them the chance to talk. This makes use of one of their most developed skills. It motivates students by giving them a space in which to think, make mistakes and share ideas. The advantages can be brought to bear at nearly any point in a lesson or they can be used in conjunction with independent writing activities.

FURTHER READING

Dewey, John (1997 [1938]). *Experience and Education* (New York: Touchstone).

Gershon, Mike (2013a). *How to Use Discussion in the Classroom: The Complete Guide* (CreateSpace).

Gershon, Mike (2013b). *How to Use Questioning in the Classroom: The Complete Guide* (CreateSpace).

Gershon, Mike (2017). *50 Quick Ways to Get Past 'I Don't Know'* (CreateSpace).

Mercer, Neil (1995). *The Guided Construction of Knowledge: Talk Amongst Teachers and Learners* (Bristol: Multilingual Matters).

Mercer, Neil (2000). *Words and Minds: How We Use Language to Think Together* (New York and Abingdon: Routledge).

Petty, Geoff (2014). *Teaching Today: A Practical Guide*, 5th edn (Oxford: Oxford University Press).

Vygotsky, Lev S. (1978). *Mind in Society: Development of Higher Psychological Processes* (Cambridge, MA: Harvard University Press).

PRACTICAL STRATEGIES

MAKING DISCUSSION ACTIVITIES
ALL-INCLUSIVE

Mike Gershon makes an important point about a significant portion of our learners who have a natural aptitude for speech over writing. To ensure that this familiar medium of communication is a learning and thinking opportunity for all, we must consider not only how we arm our learners with the skills and opportunities to verbalise their own thoughts and ideas in the classroom, but also how to share that opportunity effectively with their peers.

■ Teach your learners explicitly what it looks like and sounds like to be a good collaborator in group discussions. While basics like making eye contact with the person who is speaking, waiting for one person to finish before the next begins and ensuring that everyone has a turn to contribute seem like common sense, many of our learners need a keen reminder about this, and perhaps even clear modelling to demonstrate what this looks like. Keep the core rules available in a visible place during designated group discussion time, whether this is on a prominent classroom display or even on a card that you place on the table where learners are working.

■ Use talk tokens as a way to make discussion conventions more visible. To do this, provide each learner with a set number of tokens that will represent the number of contributions you wish each learner to make in the discussion task. The core rule for learners to remember is 'If you are speaking, you are spending'. Different types of token can be allocated to allow for contributions or questions. In this way, you are raising learners' awareness of their own discussion behaviours, as well as encouraging the skills of turn-taking, responding and bringing others into a conversation.

■ For similar impact, use a pen and a large sheet of paper to track contributions during small group discussions. The first contributor makes a dot in front of them, then the next contributor reaches out for the 'discussion pen' and draws a line (from the dot) towards himself/herself. The next person to interject then draws a line from the previous contributor's end-point towards himself/herself and so on. The result is likely to be an intricate web of lines leading back and forth between members of the group. Turn-taking is highlighted as the only person speaking is the person who is holding the pen. Learners can also see who has had an opportunity, or not, to contribute to the discussion. Learners can be encouraged to analyse their 'webs' and consider their own and their group's discussion behaviour, identifying heated exchanges, monopolisation or facilitation of talk, or even reticence to get involved at all.

- Both of the aforementioned strategies highlight for learners when there are peers in their group who have not yet been able to get involved in the group discussion. Arm your learners with strategies about what they can do to help these learners become involved in the discussion task. Asking a question, seeking an opinion or even simply a 'Hey, do you want to add anything?' can be just enough to draw more reluctant contributors into the fold.

HARNESSING THE EPHEMERAL

- Give your learners the opportunity to conduct a 'post-mortem' on an important group discussion through the use of audio recording and editing software. Once discussion time is over, ask your learners to review the audio recording and use the editing software to extract the most important ideas/contributions/phrases and create a condensed set of audio 'notes'. For interesting points that lack clarity or development, you may wish to allow them to re-record and refine for the final product. The opportunity to review, condense and refine will give your learners a chance to more carefully scrutinise and utilise the important ideas they have verbalised.

- During more extended group and paired discussion time, create 'stop and record' breaks for students to pause the discussion and note down the most important ideas or questions they have encountered so far. Not only will this give them some concrete ideas to take away and reflect on, but it can also give them a further talking point to allow discussion to develop. You might even like to appoint a 'consolidation clerk' in each group who is responsible for pausing the discussion at opportune moments and checking that all group members understand the points made. The consolidation clerk can also be in charge of asking group members to clarify contributions that might not make sense to others.

CHAPTER 17

NUDGING LEARNING

PROFESSOR MICK WATERS

During his career, PROFESSOR MICK WATERS has been a teacher and head teacher as well as working at senior levels in Birmingham and Manchester local authorities. He is an Honorary Fellow of the College of Teachers and supports several educational causes. He is a patron of the Children's University, SAPERE and the Curriculum Foundation. Mick supports the National Association for Environmental Education as a vice-president and is also chair of the CoED Foundation, which promotes compassionate education. Currently, Mick is working with the Welsh government helping to develop revised professional standards for teaching and leadership in schools.

He has written books on the curriculum, teaching and learning, and leadership, as well as making presentations at numerous national and international conferences. Mick's most recent book, *Thinking Allowed On Schooling*, was published in 2013. He is passionate about the role of education in improving life chances for pupils and works with schools on raising standards and innovative approaches to learning.

In recent times, government departments have adopted 'nudge practices' when dealing with the general public. They have found that by writing letters that are less authoritative, more personal and less demanding they get a more positive response.

Letters which are officious, threatening and forceful tend to have a less positive response than those which explain the bigger picture, describe why the issue matters and ask people to help. Income tax payment 'demands' have been more successful when the recipient is told that their money is needed for the NHS rather than being threatened with court proceedings (Halpern, 2015: 182). The number of people 'helping' goes up and the number of people 'arguing' or 'ignoring' goes down when they are reasoned with, rather than threatened with authority.

The idea is that people are 'nudged' towards the appropriate behaviour rather than being pushed or demeaned – and apparently the nudging works.

Isn't this what good schools already know and do? Good schools know that it pays to have fewer rules and apply them consistently through clear reasoning about why they matter. Good schools know that it is easier to show the benefits of rules (some call them 'understandings') to the whole community rather than threaten it with the consequences of transgression. Good schools don't need to offer complex rewards because the pupils know the logic of the way the school runs. Good schools involve pupils in decisions about their own community rather than expecting conformity with directives from the controllers.

In some schools the notion of house points is a spur to good behaviour, with pupils benefiting by accumulating points to spend on themselves. In other schools this has been developed into something much more profound by asking the pupils to offer their points to benefit one of a selection of charities. The pupils see a greater good in their own actions and feel more inclined to earn for someone beyond their own world. It is the bigger picture that educates.

Is it worth thinking about nudging in your school?

FURTHER READING

Halpern, David (2015). *Inside the Nudge Unit: How Small Changes Can Make a Big Difference* (London: WH Allen).

Waters, Mick (2013). *Thinking Allowed On Schooling* (Carmarthen: Independent Thinking Press).

PRACTICAL STRATEGIES

Simply knowing what we're expected to do is not always enough. As Mick Waters points out, sometimes we also want to know why. Having a clear understanding of why a classroom activity is important or meaningful in the long term (rather than simply 'because it's on the syllabus' or 'because I said so') can be a powerful motivator for learners. To give students this emotional buy-in to their learning, try some of these ideas.

WHY THE ISSUE MATTERS ...

■ Try sharing the learning objective with your class in the following format:

> *What* they are going to be learning (the learning objective).

> *How* they are going to be learning it (the learning activity).

> *Why* they are learning it (how it can be applied/how it will benefit them in life beyond school).

■ Try challenging learners to identify a link between the topic/skill and their personal lives. (Whether it be trigonometry or *Treasure Island*, with careful consideration it is always possible to establish some sort of connection

between the subject matter and their life events, their
interests or their family history!)

NUDGING PEOPLE TOWARDS APPROPRIATE BEHAVIOURS FOR LEARNING

Nudging need not be a top-down process. Giving learners a purposeful forum to discuss the tenets of great learning can be the perfect way to step away from consequence-driven rules about classroom conduct. Making the link between behaviour for learning and good outcomes will help to nudge learners in the right direction.

- To make explicit what best practice looks like, nominate several learners to act as 'classroom paparazzi'. Once clear success criteria are established and the class is set off on a task, the job of the paparazzi is to use photographic equipment to catch their peers in the act: what does it look like to be engaged and learning in this lesson? If learners have been set a collaborative task, what does good collaboration look like? If specific resources have been provided, how can they best be deployed? What does it look like to help your peers? What does it look like to persevere?

Over the course of the activity, the paparazzi need to gather evidence that the success criteria, both in terms of output and behaviour for learning, have been applied. The paparazzi can capture both stills and short video clips of the 'best learning' in progress. The job of the paparazzi at the end of the lesson is to debrief their findings and share their most useful images and clips with the class. Using classroom paparazzi raises learners' awareness about their participation and playfully nudges them towards greater engagement in the activity. The discussion afterwards can provide a great forum for peer assessment.

INVOLVING PEOPLE IN DECISIONS ABOUT THEIR COMMUNITY

It is always easy to gather the thoughts and feelings of the willing, but is this representative of the whole? How can we encourage the reticent to come forward with their questions, ideas or concerns? How can we ensure that the loudest or most frequent voices are not the only ones that get consideration? Consider the following two techniques as possible ways to level the playing field when gathering opinions from your learners.

■ When looking to gather opinion in a pastoral setting, first share the topic of query with the class (extra-curricular clubs they would like to see, changes to the school uniform, improvements to school dinners, homework, etc.).

Give each learner a piece of paper to record their thoughts on the topic. Next, assign an appropriate time parameter (30-60 seconds is usually plenty) to come up with an initial response to the query itself. This might be a further question, a comment, an idea or solution, an identified flaw and so on. Once the time parameter has expired, the learners must pass their piece of paper to a peer, who is then given a block of time to add or respond to their peer's initial notes. When that block of time has expired, the pieces of paper are passed again to further classmates, and the process is repeated as many times as the teacher deems productive. The notes that have, by now, been shared, reconsidered and developed several times over can then be passed back to the teacher for perusal. A further task could be set requiring the learners to summarise the findings on the last note they received. Alternatively, they could get together in small groups and compile the findings of a selection of notes.

■ Keep parents and carers engaged in school life by placing a 'parent voice' box in a prominent place which can be easily accessed by them. By placing plenty of carefully designed suggestion forms (and a pen) next to the box, you can prevent people from writing long unhelpful rants and encourage them instead to be solution focused. Make sure that they are obliged to include their name and contact details so that all suggestions can be responded to by the school.

CHAPTER 18

NEXT STEPS ...

TEACHER DEVELOPMENT TRUST

A school that engages teachers, students and the wider community is one that is most likely to achieve excellent outcomes for their learning. We need teachers who are skilled, confident practitioners in engaging their classes and engaging with parents. But if teachers are going to learn *about* engagement, then we certainly need that learning process itself to be engaging!

When students are engaged in their learning, they're focused, they're motivated and they're thinking hard. In this chapter we explore further the theme of engagement in schools: how teachers can explore it and how senior leaders can create time and support for professional learning. As some of the contributors in this book have highlighted, an engaging approach to CPD can allow teachers to develop their knowledge and practice to best meet students' needs. Done right, we can design professional learning that really helps pupils succeed and teachers thrive.

RELEVANCE AND PURPOSE

One of the most common barriers to engagement in professional learning activities is a feeling of irrelevance – 'This is nice, but I've got more important issues to deal with.' Teachers are very busy people and we don't appreciate being made to sit through presentations that don't feel helpful.

But it's not just about whether it *feels* relevant. Research shows that professional learning is much more likely to have an impact on student outcomes if it is explicitly and closely linked to our students' needs (Teacher Development Trust, 2015). Too often development opportunities are tied to accountability or performance management. That can feel a long way away from the reason why we got into the profession and why we put in all of the day-to-day effort with our students.

Student-focused professional learning should include:

■ A diagnosis of students' needs to help identify an area of focus – 'What do I need them to learn?' or 'What barriers do I need to overcome to help them learn?'

■ Linking a strategy or an evidence-informed approach to this student need – 'What's the best thing for me to learn that would most likely help here?'

■ Ongoing experimentation, where teachers are constantly engaged in evaluating whether or not the strategy is meeting students' needs – 'Am I making a difference yet? How can I improve this strategy further?'

To make this possible, we need to feel some sense of ownership over our professional learning and ensure that it is designed to engage and inspire our learners' specific needs. While school leaders are in a position to identify common trends across schoolwide data, teachers and support staff are the ones on the 'front line' working directly with students, parents and the community. As such, they are best placed to identify students' detailed needs and diagnose the detail behind broader trends.

For example, when a class seemingly underperforms in their English exams compared to the statistical estimates, this doesn't tell us enough about *why*. What are the barriers? Where are the specific areas of difficulty? Ultimately, what work do teachers need to do to improve? A CPD programme needs to take into account teachers' own diagnoses of the issues if it is going to feel engaging to them.

The best CPD programmes give space not only for whole-school training but also for CPD within teams (e.g. phase teams, subject teams, year teams). It also takes account of staff members' performance management goals and career plans, giving a range of opportunities for everyone to feel that they are being developed.

Tip for teachers: in your next team meeting, bring a scheme of work or lesson plan for a topic that you will all be teaching shortly. Consider which practical strategies in this book will most complement the subject matter and skills you will need to cover. Once you have made a careful selection, you can begin to plan when you will trial each technique.

Tip for leaders: give teachers time to interview small focus groups of students to ask them about which lessons feel most engaging, and encourage teachers to give careful consideration to the responses they collect.

BUILDING ENGAGEMENT AMONG STAFF

Too often, professional learning is a one-off activity, seemingly 'done to' teachers by leaders or out-of-touch external speakers who don't take the time to ascertain the audience's genuine needs. This is often the least effective professional learning and, the research would suggest, is unlikely to have an impact (Teacher Development Trust, 2015). However, the other extreme is every teacher choosing all of their own CPD, following whatever they feel interested in at the time. Where on the spectrum do we see the greatest engagement *and* the greatest impact?

Conscripts vs. volunteers

The TDT's review, *Developing Great Teaching* (2015), gives a surprising finding: the best student outcomes are not necessarily achieved when teachers are given completely free individual choice over CPD. Sometimes the best professional learning can start with some participants feeling sceptical, but they buy in along the way. In other circumstances, the most effective CPD can involve compromise – what's best for developing our collective expertise rather than working on lots of projects individually?

The priority for teacher engagement in professional learning should therefore not always be to offer ever more options and choices. Therein lies the danger of the 'shoal of fish' syndrome – everyone swimming around very fast and looking very busy but the whole organisation moving nowhere. A great CPD programme needs some coherence, with some key priorities sustained over one or more years and many teams working on each of them. There's still room for individual menus, but it's balanced with team and whole-school priorities.

Tip for teachers: take some time in a team meeting or in informal discussions to explore the common barriers to engagement that the whole team is facing in your key stage, subject or specialism. What have been the engagement success stories – which parents or students had the biggest breakthroughs, and why? How could you all work together to get more success? In order to move forward, identify which of the identified barriers and successes would require support from SLT/whole-school systems, and which are feasible to tackle within your team?

Innovation and risk taking

An important part of professional learning is the opportunity to experiment with your practice and to take risks. Solving problems and trying new things feels engaging! Nothing works in every context, so teachers need the support to try things out and learn from them, even if they don't work.

Too often we see teachers engage in some professional learning but not actually make any change to their practice because they don't have the time, they don't have the resources or they're too cautious of changing anything in case it doesn't work. Leaders should model their own learning and their own innovation, and where teachers experiment and try out new ideas, this should also be celebrated and recognised. It is just as important to learn what *doesn't* work and to share this.

Tip for leaders: could you stick a sign on your door saying, 'This term, I'm learning about ...' or 'This term, I'm working on ...'?

PRIORITISING PROFESSIONAL LEARNING

If you have experienced ineffective professional learning, you are much more likely to be put off engaging in it again. Sadly, many teachers will probably have experienced ineffective CPD at some point in their career. It is important to communicate its benefit for both teachers *and* students. As soon as things are busy in a school (which is most of the time), it is tempting to drop the long-term developmental tasks in favour of the immediate, urgent ones. However, if leaders can show they are willing to flex other demands and deadlines to retain space for CPD, it sends an important signal about the extent to which CPD is valuable.

Tip for leaders: at the start of the year, identify one or two potentially unnecessary or superfluous meetings/briefings that you could possibly shorten (or even skip completely) to release more time for CPD.

PROVIDING TIME

The most common issue around professional learning is finding time. Time and money are often in short supply. Yet professional learning cannot just be an add-on, and we know it is too important to be something that is not prioritised because of time constraints. Where staff have space to reflect and develop and, crucially, see that it is a priority for the school, they are much more likely to engage fully.

Below are some options to consider for finding time for teachers to engage in professional learning:

- Bank regular professional development time by finishing school lessons slightly later on most days and then using that time for one day a week or fortnight for professional learning (e.g. pupils arrive later than usual or leave earlier than usual; this is more common at secondary level).

- Schedule music, sport, art, reading sessions and/or religious education with specialist external facilitators to free up time for collaboration or development.

- Use assembly times with fewer staff and/or teaching assistants and external facilitators.

- Extend departmental meeting times and use these for collaboration time. Minimise any administrative tasks and communication in this time.

- Disaggregate statutory INSET days; instead use the time for several twilight or dawn sessions.

- Preserve statutory INSET day time for co-planning and discussion.

- Keep a ruthless focus on workload and remove anything that is taking up time but not benefitting students sufficiently (e.g. excessive written comments when giving feedback, frequent and repetitive data entry, extraneous paperwork around lesson planning).

Tip for teachers: can you and your team all agree to an email pledge? If the key administrative points for the meeting can be summarised in an email that all members of the department read beforehand, then the time gained can be spent focusing on teaching and learning rather than relaying information.

PROVIDING RESOURCES

Effective and engaging professional learning needs to include support and new perspectives from external experts. This might be anything from a sustained relationship with a researcher in a university, some whole-school or departmental input from a particular engaging and celebrated expert or a visit to another school. These external perspectives help to provide new ways of thinking. If school leaders are seen to invest in this, teachers are much more likely to engage.

Tip for leaders: give several (or even all) staff a morning or afternoon to visit another school. Teachers can bring back ideas about engagement and use those ideas and the practical strategies in this book to develop a year-long engagement project.

FURTHER READING

Coe, Robert, Aloisi, Cesare, Higgins, Steve and Major, Lee Elliot (2014). *What Makes Great Teaching? Review of the Underpinning Research* (London: Sutton Trust). Available at: http://www. suttontrust.com/researcharchive/great-teaching/.

Department for Education (2016). *Standard for Teachers' Professional Development* (London: Department for Education). Available at: https://www.gov.uk/government/publications/ standard-for-teachers-professional-development.

Teacher Development Trust (2015). *Developing Great Teaching: Lessons from the International Reviews Into Effective Professional Development* (London: Teacher Development Trust). Available at: http://TDTrust.org/about/dgt.

Timperley, Helen, Wilson, Aaron, Barrar, Heather and Fung, Irene (2007). *Teacher Professional Learning and Development: Best Evidence Synthesis Iteration (BES)* (Wellington: Ministry of Education). Available at: https://www.educationcounts.govt.nz/ publications/series/2515/15341.

ALSO AVAILABLE

BEST OF THE BEST:
PROGRESS

BEST OF THE BEST:
FEEDBACK

**UPCOMING TITLE
IN THIS SERIES**

BEST OF THE BEST:
DIFFERENTIATION

World-class experts, important ideas, practical strategies

🐦 Follow the conversation at #BOTB

BEST OF THE BEST
PROGRESS

ISBN: 978-178583160-7

BEST OF THE BEST

FEEDBACK

ISBN: 978-178583187-4

BEST
OF THE
BEST
PRACTICAL
CLASSROOM GUIDES

DYLAN WILIAM
ART COSTA
ROBERT GARMSTON
BILL LUCAS
DIANA LAUFENBERG
PAUL DIX
TAYLOR MALI
RON BERGER

FEEDBACK

ANDY GRIFFITH
BARRY HYMER
JACKIE BEERE
MIKE GERSHON
MICK WATERS
GEOFF PETTY
SHIRLEY CLARKE
SETH GODIN
PHIL BEADLE

ISABELLA WALLACE AND LEAH KIRKMAN